Blood Brothers

Blood Brothers

THE BIOGRAPHY OF *THE VAMPIRE DIARIES'* IAN SOMERHALDER

AMY RICKMAN

JOHN BLAKE

Published by John Blake Publishing Ltd,
3 Bramber Court, 2 Bramber Road,
London W14 9PB, England

www.johnblakepublishing.co.uk

www.facebook.com/Johnblakepub facebook
twitter.com/johnblakepub twitter

First published in paperback in 2011

ISBN: 978 1 84358 410 0

British Library Cataloguing-in-Publication Data:

A catalogue record for this book is available from the British Library.

Design by www.envydesign.co.uk

Printed in Great Britain by CPI Bookmarque, CR0 4TD

1 3 5 7 9 10 8 6 4 2

Papers used by John Blake Publishing are natural, recyclable products made from wood grown in sustainable forests. The manufacturing processes conform to the environmental regulations of the country of origin.

Every attempt has been made to contact the relevant copyright-holders, but some were unobtainable. We would be grateful if the appropriate people could contact us.

Contents

Acknowledgements

Many thanks to my editor Joel Simons and the entire John Blake publishing team – writing this book has been a blast and I always appreciate your support. Other thanks must go to my parents, who were hooked on this show before I'd even heard of it; to my sister, because it took vampires to make her love reading; to Sarah, for being my biggest advocate and closest friend; and finally to Lofty, for watching every episode and putting up with me as I blurted out random *The Vampire Diaries'* facts constantly and without warning.

Spoiler Alert!

Hi, *The Vampire Diaries'* fans!

I've paid extra attention to make sure that you aren't spoiled for Season Two but if you haven't watched Season One yet, beware that there might be a spoiler ahead. So what are you waiting for? There are two delicious brothers just dying for your blood!

Ian Somerhalder

*

Damon Salvatore

Introduction

The mist is rising. Somewhere, close by, a raven caws. A slow chill begins to creep up your spine – whether from the sudden cold in the air or the eeriness of the scene, you're not sure. It occurs to you that a midnight stroll through a graveyard might not have been such a good idea.

A twig snaps, bird wings flutter. It's almost impossible to hear anything over the beating of your own heart. Did something just move in the shadows?

You feel the sudden heat of breath on your shoulder. Now you remember why you came here, to this place, to this graveyard with its broken tombstones and creeping vines: you came to learn more about one of the brothers – but which one will it be?

You spin around and out of nowhere one of them has appeared. Tonight, it's Damon Salvatore. His piercing bright blue eyes have you weak at the knees; his lopsided bad-boy smile sets you to trembling. Yes, he is the one you wanted.

Lucky for you, Damon has a little time tonight. He is always willing to talk about his favourite subject – himself – before he gets too hungry to resist taking a bite out of you.

There's no turning back now…

Chapter One

Ian's Green Beginnings

Damon: I'm here to eat cotton candy – and to steal your girl.
(1.22, 'Founder's Day')

The first thing everyone notices about Ian Somerhalder is his startling eyes: they're deep blue and piercing, almost magnetic, and they immediately set him apart from the pack. 'He can look you in the eyes and make you do whatever he wants,' says Julie Plec, one of the creators of *The Vampire Diaries*. Ian even has a nickname among his cast-mates that is especially appropriate: 'Smolderholder' so it's hardly a surprise that this gorgeous man from the Deep South of the USA has ended up playing the sexiest of all monsters, the undead seductor: a vampire.

It helped as well that he grew up in the homeland of vampire authoress extraordinaire Anne Rice (author of *Interview With The Vampire* and creator of one of the greatest vampire characters of all time, Lestat). Ian's home lay just across

Lake Pontchartrain from New Orleans in Mandeville, Louisiana. It's a place known for its rich history, gothic atmosphere and mythical creations: 'I grew up on the lake in New Orleans, on the north shore, in a more rural area, and I could look across the lake and see New Orleans. I remember always thinking, "There's vampires over there."' Not that Ian would ever admit to being scared, not even as a child. 'Sometimes we'd go over there when I was a little kid, and it wasn't that it was scary, but it was enticing. It was the not-knowing. Now that I'm on [*The Vampire Diaries*], it's cool to go back there and see it. I thought, "Wow, I used to look at that skyline from 26 miles away, across this huge lake, and think, Are the vampires going to get me, mom and dad?"'

Of course they would come to get him – but not quite yet! There were still many years to go before Ian would cease to wonder about vampires and start becoming one.

Ian was born Ian Joseph Somerhalder on 8 December 1978 in Covington, Louisiana, and he is the middle sibling between his older brother, Robert (better known as Bob) and his younger sister, Robyn. Both of Ian's siblings have gone on to have successful careers of their own – Bob was a professional cyclist and Robyn worked in broadcast journalism. Ian didn't have the same kind of sibling rivalry with Bob that his character Damon has with Stefan, though: 'There wasn't much rivalry,' he told *Metro*. 'My brother was seven years older so he just kicked my ass.'

His dad, Robert Somerhalder senior, worked as an independent building contractor and his mother, Edna, was a massage therapist from Mississippi who grew up on a pig farm! It's obvious that Ian's good looks come from the unique mixture of his background: his dad can claim English and French heritage, while his mother is Irish and part-Choctaw Native American.

The Somerhalders have a really interesting family mythology surrounding their last name. They can trace their history right back to their biological great-grandfather, who was a wealthy landowner in England with the surname Hull. He had an affair, and when the woman fell pregnant he didn't want to deal with the consequences. Instead he decided to pay off one of his immigrant workers to marry the mistress and take the baby far away. The worker's last name was 'Somerhalder' and the rest is history.

Ian's parents divorced when he was fourteen and he lived with his mum. Edna was a very spiritual person, who sent her children to Catholic school and gave them herbal medicinal remedies when they got sick before giving them Western pharmaceuticals, part of the legacy of Ian's Native-American grandmother. Edna is very health-conscious and taught her kids proper nutrition and how to eat healthily and organically; these were the values she instilled in her son from an early age and he has continued to follow them. According to him, his mother 'made my baby food and had me on blue-green algae probably since I was in third grade. I never had sugar, I never got to have white bread or any white-flour products.' Indeed, his only indulgence was a slice of chocolate cake on his birthday. Even now he maintains healthy eating standards such as drinking between three and ten cups of green tea every day, his favourite being Jasmine Pearl tea.

Like any kid, Ian sometimes yearned for the treats that his classmates got to have. One day at elementary school, during lunch hour, he looked down at his über-healthy sandwich (said to be grilled vegetables on marble rye bread), compared it to his friend's lunch of peanut butter-and-jelly smeared between two layers of white bread, and felt a twinge of envy so he asked for a trade. He would never make that mistake again. The sugar-and-preservative laden lunch made him sick to his stomach. 'I can't eat fast food... I haven't eaten McDonald's in ten years. I eat fish every day,' he explains.

Even more than eating healthily, Ian's mum also taught her family to live healthily and encouraged Ian and his siblings to go out and enjoy the great outdoors. His favourite toy was a red BB gun (a kind of air gun) that he would take out among the marshes and fields around his house to play games. He must've gotten up to lots of high jinks with that gun as he wouldn't give one to his own children: 'I grew up in the country and would I give a child (I mean a six- to nine-year-old) a gun? Absolutely, without a doubt, hell no!'

The rich cultural history surrounding New Orleans also enabled the energetic Ian to release some energy as he used to participate in reenactments of the American Civil War, where he would dress up in eighteenth-century costume and run around a fake battlefield. Little did he know this would be the perfect practice for a role to come!

Ian also found fuel in his father's stories. Robert Somerhalder had served in the military during the Vietnam War but it wasn't his tales of warfare that Ian found appealing, but the adventure and travel in South-East Asia that his father had experienced. It made Ian realise the world was so much bigger than Louisiana and he wanted to travel and see it all: 'I've had these feelings since I was a kid... Ever since I can remember, I've wanted to travel to new cities, new hotel rooms – I should have been a damn rock star.'

Ian's ambition and thirst for life steadily grew as he experienced more and more: 'I had a great [childhood]. We had horses and motorcycles and boats, but I always wanted more – a bigger horse or a faster bike or whatever,' he recalls. Being greedy was not a value that Edna wanted to encourage and besides, the family didn't have the money to give Ian all he wanted; instead, his mother wanted him to learn that the only way to achieve your goals and get what you want is through hard work. Edna suggested that Ian get a job as a model, so he could work and earn some money. She knew some people in the business and Ian was keen: 'I said, "Sure, sign me up!"' His mother then scrimped and saved so they could rent an apartment in New York for three summers. It worked, though, as Ian landed a three-year contract with Ford Modeling Agency in New York, 'and I was making more money an hour than people with PhDs.' He was only ten years old at the time.

And so it was that in the summertime, when most kids went to camp or were away on holiday, Ian went to New York to model, with his mum as his manager. Almost immediately he started to get bookings for big-name clients, his first being for Ralph Lauren: he modelled their kids' range, becoming one of the company's 'little polo boys'. As he told Jay Leno on *The Tonight Show*: 'It was a blast, it was so fun.' Other modelling jobs quickly followed, for Calvin Klein, American Eagle Outfitters, Dolce & Gabbana, Gucci and Versace. The experience was to change him for life: 'I was exposed to a lot of interesting things, talented photographers and cool intellectuals, and New York City got into my blood. It was a juxtaposition of New York and this quiet, rural area of Louisiana my family lived in. It changes your outlook on childhood – you grow up really fast.'

In fact, Ian was so successful as a model that by the time he turned thirteen and started at junior high, he was already pretty burned out of the fashion world. He took some time off to focus on his studies, sports and his friends back home. Like many successful teens who balanced school with modelling (and soon, acting), he often felt ostracised at high school and wasn't part of any particular group. He didn't let it bother him though, as he knew he was destined for great things beyond school. And so to make the most of his time there, he joined the high school's drama society and focused on working towards his dream. 'I was just "me" in high school,' says Ian on his website. 'If anything, [and it's] my motto still, ... I didn't care what others thought/think of me, to be honest. I was doing the whole modeling thing at that point and caught tons of shit because of it. If you do what you love (music, art, sports, writing, academics, etc.), who cares what or whom is deemed as "rejected" you know? As long as you aren't hurting anyone and obeying your parents for the most part, as well as obeying the law for the most part, who cares who is "rejected"! I was a reject at times, sure – we all are!'

Ian's hiatus from the big city worked for a little while, but it seemed as if New York wouldn't leave him alone. The agencies, designers and photographers all wanted him back – and this time as an adult star. The week after he turned sixteen, he left his Louisiana home to live permanently in New York and pursue his modelling career. This meant going through a complicated process called 'emancipation' – where a minor (i.e. someone under the age of eighteen) leaves home in order to pursue a business or occupation without the involvement or approval of their parents. 'I left home a week after I turned sixteen and started working,' Ian told *Tribune*. 'My parents trusted me. There's a whole emancipation process where you can live on your own – we just had this understanding that it was OK. Now I look back and go, "Wow – sixteen!" But when you have agents who make sure you're driven around the city, you're protected; you have someone to watch out for you.'

And this time it wasn't just going to be New York for Ian: he had a new manager, a woman he considered his surrogate mother called Brenda Netzberger, and with Brenda and Ford Models (and later DNA Models), he travelled all over the world – from New York and Los Angeles to Paris, London, Barcelona and Milan. For Ian, it felt like a dream come true and he quickly realised that one of his passions was travelling and exploring – he loved being opened up to new cultures.

Living in Europe was an incredible growing-up experience for Ian and he soon found himself immersed in a world he didn't always understand: 'I went off the rails and down the side of the mountain. I went nuts for a while, but I soon grew out of it,' he told *Metro*. 'Kids in Europe go crazy at a slower pace than kids in America. There are things that are accepted in Europe that aren't in America: you can drink at 16 in Europe, kids have a good time, but it's not like in the States when you have to wait until you're 21, end up pounding a case of beer in one night and end up in hospital – kids don't need to do that in Europe.'

More big fashion names continued to fall over themselves to hire him and Versace was his first massive campaign: 'Versace was my first campaign as an adult (meaning it was after modelling when I was ten to thirteen) at sixteen. It was shot in Massachusetts with Bruce Weber and basically kicked off, what I guess for lack of better words, this "journey" if you will. It was that week or so that would introduce me to the individuals whom I would be seeing, travelling with, partying with and doing some very crazy, not-so-legal activities in the company of over the coming years.'

Modelling took him to some amazing places. One of his best memories was of a shoot in Mexico. He was shooting with a photographer named Ken Browar and a female model when they had to hike deep into the jungle in order to get to the specific location. On arrival, they were treated to an incredible wildlife encounter: 'While shooting and learning about this area of the country, we venture up a steep mountain to a magical place where the Monarch butterflies migrate every year. Hiking into some enchanted forest at an elevation I couldn't tell you, but high – you find yourself on a grassy plain, asking yourself: "Where are the damn butterflies?" Upon turning around I saw and will never forget: the entire tree line was moving. So many butterflies that the branches sagged, imagine that! You could walk into the trees and be greeted by thousands of them, dancing all over you – an unbelievable experience!'

Modelling was certainly taking Ian around the world and setting him up financially, but he still wanted to pursue his other passion – acting. 'Modelling was lucrative but not intellectually satisfying,' he told Copley News Service. When he was seventeen, he enrolled in some acting classes and by nineteen he knew he had the bug. His very first experience on a set was in 1997, for a TV series called *The Big Easy*, based in New Orleans. 'Showing up on set… I kept looking at the matte-box [the device used to prevent glare on a camera lens], and the director kept saying: "Don't look in the camera, don't look in the camera." And I thought, "What am I doing, I know not to do that." … When I look back on that I laugh, hysterically,' he told *Newsweek*. To improve his craft, he worked with acting coach William Esper and he was learning with the best. Esper is one of the most pre-eminent acting teachers in the world. He has worked with many famous faces, including *Sex and the City*'s Kristin Davis, Aaron Eckhart (*The Dark Knight, Thank You For Smoking*) and Kim Basinger (*L.A. Confidential*). While he continued to model to make money and pay the rent, he began turning up for auditions as well. But it wasn't until he got spotted in a crowded room that he really started to make it big.

Chapter Two

Model-Turned-Actor

Damon: Your life was pathetic. Your after-life doesn't have to be. (1.07, 'Haunted')

In interviews, Ian comes off as surprisingly self-conscious about his very traditional career trajectory: 'Models-turned-actors are a bit of a cliché,' he told *Metro*. 'It is a huge cliché but you have to look at the positive aspects – I learned a lot about the world and took a lot of knowledge away from it.'

It was now the late nineties and Ian had just turned twenty. He was on the set of a feature film called *Black and White* (1999) starring Robert Downey Jr. and Elijah Wood, about a group of white high-school students who get involved in a predominantly black Harlem hip-hop scene. Ian was only an extra – one club-goer among a 400-strong crowd, but he clearly stood out from the group. He was spotted by a talent manager who signed him up right away.

From then on, the acting jobs came thick and fast. It must

have been fate – Ian did four auditions and booked all of them. After his *The Big Easy* experience, and a brief stint on a short-lived TV series called *Now and Again*, Ian got a part in a spin-off of *Dawson's Creek* – the series that launched *The Vampire Diaries*' creator Kevin Williamson's career. The show was called *Young Americans* and followed Will Krudski (introduced briefly on *Dawson's Creek* as one of Pacey J. Witter's childhood friends) as he starts at an exclusive American all-boys' boarding school. Ian's character was Hamilton Fleming, the son of the dean. Hamilton is confused about his sexuality and thinks he's falling in love with a fellow student. It turns out though that the student is actually a girl disguised as a boy. The series also launched the career of another teen star, Kate Bosworth (*Blue Crush* and *Superman Returns*).

This wasn't to be the only time when Ian played a character confused by his sexuality. In fact, it seemed to be a bit of a theme in his body of work pre-Lost and *The Vampire Diaries*. In his next two roles, he played bisexual characters. The first was in a TV movie called *My Life as a House*, a tear-jerking drama about George Monroe (Kevin Kline), a man with terminal cancer who struggles to reach out to his estranged son, Sam (played by a pre-Star Wars' Hayden Christensen). Ian played Josh, a hustler, pimp, drug dealer and all-around bad guy who tries to turn Sam to a life of drugs and prostitution. '[*My Life as a House*] was the first studio film I was part of, and it was amazing. I remember, after some takes, Kevin Kline would just walk around singing,' he told TV Mania. The movie was well reviewed and although Ian's role in it was small, he helped bring some edge to an otherwise overly saccharine drama.

The second role was his biggest to date: he was cast as Paul Denton in an adaptation of Bret Easton Ellis's novel *The Rules of Attraction* by director Roger Avary, alongside James Van Der

Beek and Jessica Biel. The movie was a dark satire about college life, depicting three main characters and their disassociation with their outrageous sex lives. It was highly controversial when it came out in 2002 and completely divided critics – the BBC described it as 'fiercely original and seriously funny' while respected movie reviewers Ebert & Roeper simply said they 'hated this movie.' The film was originally given an NC-17 rating in the US – one of the highest ratings available – and awarded an 18+ in the UK, yet most of the controversy came from Somerhalder himself. He and James Van Der Beek had to kiss during a scene where Paul (Ian's character) fantasises about a sexual experience with Sean (Van Der Beek). Somerhalder spoke to *A&F* magazine about the kiss: 'Here is the thing: Two guys kissing is not as sexy as two girls kissing. When Selma Blair made out with Sarah-what's-her-name [in *Cruel Intentions*], that was hot. Me and James Van Der Beek making out is not hot, it's rather disgusting. We both looked at each other and said, "Dude, don't stick your tongue in my mouth."'

Naturally, those comments spread through the media like wildfire until Ian finally had to come out and defend himself against accusations of homophobia. 'It's not me who can't handle it, it's the audience. Seann William Scott didn't get all of the backlash that I received when he did just the same in *American Pie 2*. It was completely unjustified – fans and outraged men saying that I was making anti-gay remarks. I wasn't and those very close to me who are gay were visibly upset. I'd never make a disrespectful remark about anyone, especially in public, about one's sexual preference.'

Furthermore, he felt victimised by the journalist who had, as far as he was concerned, twisted his words to make a sensational story. For three years, from 2003–2005, he kept up a series of mini-interviews called the Friday Five on his official website.

When a fan questioned him about the journalist's story, on his Friday Five he wrote: 'Most of my dearest friends in the world are homosexual men and women. Having said that I can honestly say that I have a great understanding of them and appreciate them for all that they are and give to my and the world around them. It's easy for someone to make me look as though I say negative things about people who are gay. I would say that they are wrong. Never have I said anything derogatory but instead have done nothing but support and work for organizations that support gay rights and many others.'

The film itself might have divided critics, but the author of the novel, Brett Easton Ellis, was happy. Four of his works have been adapted into movies (*Less Than Zero* [1987], *American Psycho* [2000], *The Rules of Attraction* [2002], and *The Informers* [2008]), and he considers *The Rules of Attraction* to be the best: 'My favourite movie out of the four was *The Rules of Attraction.* I thought it was the only one that captured the sensibility of the novel in a cinematic way. I know I'm sounding like a film critic on that, but I'm talking about that in an emotional [way] – as the writer of the novel. I watched that movie and thought they got it in a way that Mary Harron [director of *American Psycho*] didn't and *Less Than Zero* didn't.'

Even before he had experienced it himself, Ian knew a little about victimisation from another movie he had starred in, called *Anatomy of a Hate Crime* (2001), which chronicled the real-life story of the torture and murder of twenty-one-year-old gay college student Matthew Shepard. Ian played one of Matthew's murderers, Russell Henderson. The film focused as much on the twisted motivations of his killers as it did on Matthew and it was broadcast on MTV in three half-hour acts as part of their year-long drive: 'Fight For Your Rights: Take A Stand Against Discrimination'. It was probably the role that had most affected him up until then, as he wrote on his Friday Five: 'I have to say after *Anatomy of a Hate Crime* (the movie wasn't great, though), I truly understood that one's life can change in a matter of moments...'

The Friday Five was very important to Ian, who was keen to connect with his fans in a different way to most actors. He really didn't consider himself 'famous' at that point, but he did have a steady fan base that he wanted to keep in touch with. Every week he would answer five questions, ranging from the very personal to the professional, and with virtually no subject off-limits – from shows to relationships to philosophy. It was there that fans learned about his relationship with American socialite Nicky Hilton (and the subsequent break-up); Ian even kept the Friday Five going when his career started to take off and he landed the part of Boone Carlyle on *Lost* – showing that his growing celebrity had not affected his down-to-earth nature.

The following years Ian spent building up his résumé on the small screen, with frequent guest spots on popular television shows such as *Law & Order: Special Victims Unit* and *CSI: Miami*. He then landed a recurring guest-star role on *Smallville* as Adam Knight, a teenager who died from a liver disease but was later resurrected using a special injection known as 'Lazarus Serum'. Adam was sent to *Smallville* by Lex Luthor's father Lionel to befriend Lana Lang and spy on Clark Kent. Altogether, Ian shot six episodes before his character died from lack of serum to keep him 'undead' ending his time on the hit show.

It was 2004 and Ian was in need of a big role... and soon he was about to crash-land into the perfect one.

Chapter Three

The Lost Years

Damon: This town needs a bit of a wake-up call, don't you think? (1.02, 'The Night of the Comet')

Ian was being picky. He wanted a major role, but he didn't want to do just any old movie or television show that came along. Yet when Brenda Netzberger, his manager, called, desperate to show him a script, he knew better than to dismiss her opinion – they had been working together for too long for that. 'I actually didn't want to read pilots,' said Ian on a Friday Five, 'but my manager told me that she was sending a few pages from a pilot and that I should look at the director and the location. Upon following the instructions from her, I immediately called her after seeing that it was J.J. Abrams and it shot in Hawaii!'

For Ian, the decision was made before he had even properly found out about the role. J.J. (Jeffrey Jacob) Abrams had a great track record with television shows (before *Lost*, he worked on

Felicity and *Alias*) and an incredible reputation in Hollywood as the hottest young director, writer and producer on the scene. Ian headed out straightaway to meet with him and the other executive producers.

It was a rigorous process but a relatively straightforward one for Ian. He filmed a few audition scenes in front of a camera, which were then viewed by the network and studio for approval. Luckily, right from the beginning J.J. believed in him. Ian described a particular moment in the audition process on his website:

> In a screening room that resembles a small theatre at ABC (and trust me, a network test is a very intense room to be in) the silence was perfect so that concentration was never broken. By that time J.J. and myself had been in several meetings together for the role with Damon [Lindelof, executive producer] so those guys were on my team, my champions on the project, so needless to say that trust and comfort yields a fearlessness in you that allows you to live an organic moment in an artificial environment.
>
> The last part of the test was the scene with Boone and Sawyer (was never put into the final draft of the pilot) in which Boone was digging for something in the sand while Sawyer sat smoking (of course) watching Boone only to make some smart-ass comment (of course) while Boone calmly and articulately put Sawyer in his place. I'll never forget, when that scene was done I literally thought that I was on a beach somewhere talking to this guy and upon realizing that it was indeed a room; there was more silence. I looked up at J.J. and he simply said to the executives behind him – 'As I live and breathe, ladies and gentlemen, Ian Somerhalder.'

For that one moment and many, many more that followed, I thank you, Mr. Abrams.

With that stellar audition, Ian was the first actor to be announced on the cast of *Lost* in early 2004 – as Boone Carlyle. The character really intrigued him: Boone was part of the original group of survivors from the middle section of the plane, alongside main characters Jack, Kate, Sawyer and Locke (among others). Before the crash he had been a wealthy young man, whose mother owned a wedding company. Boone became the chief operating officer of his mother's company when he turned twenty; he also had a stepsister named Shannon, whom he had romantic feelings towards, and he was very protective of her. His character was described in a *USA Today* profile as 'a callow young man who had been toughened by island challenges.' Boone was also incredibly vain, so much so that his sister sarcastically labels him: 'God's Friggin' Gift to Humanity' (that could be accurately used to describe Ian as well, though not in a sarcastic way!).

Ready to take on the challenge, Ian flew out to Hawaii in March, 2004 and watched as the cast grew and began to draw in more big-name stars and attractive unknowns with oodles of potential. One actor he immediately clicked with was Dominic Monaghan, who was cast as Charlie. Monaghan was riding high after successfully starring in Peter Jackson's *The Lord of the Rings* films as the hobbit, Merry. Ian chatted with him about his experience on *The Lord of the Rings'* set, especially as he himself had actually auditioned for a part in the hit movies: 'Few people know that, but I auditioned for the role of Legolas,' he told *Séries* magazine in France. 'Unfortunately, it didn't work out. Orlando Bloom was stronger than me on this! [laughs]

When Dominic tells me about the wonderful experience he's had on the set, I regret that I didn't get the role but in this job, we can't win first prize all the time.'

He also got on really well with his on-screen sister, Shannon, played by Maggie Grace. Ian described her as: 'hateable in *Lost*, but really she's the sweetest, most adorable thing on the planet.' Immediately rumours started to fly that the two were dating, but both denied it.

However, the person on-set that Ian got along with best was also the one he truly envied. That person was Josh Holloway, otherwise known as James 'Sawyer' Ford. Like almost every other male member of the cast, Ian had originally wanted to play the part of bad-boy Sawyer. 'I was always so envious of Josh Holloway on *Lost* because he always gets to say the cool stuff. And it's always so fun to watch, even if it's someone you don't necessarily like, you still want to hear what they have to say and the way they say it. They truly mean what they're saying, even if it's demented and wrong.'

Even now, long after Ian's time on *Lost* has ended, he and Josh have remained good friends. They have even gone shopping together, with Ian helping his friend to pick out a post-pregnancy gift for his wife: 'Ian helped me pick out chick shoes and we ended up getting tanked and having a blast,' Josh told *TV Guide*. Ian picked up the story: 'Just imagine me and Josh, two macho dudes, after a couple bottles of wine, walking through Nordstrom's shoe department, discussing the types of heels, toes and colour.'

Despite being located on the beautiful, sun-soaked islands of Hawaii, the shooting was tough. 'It was really intense,' Ian revealed to TV Mania. 'You're covered in bug spray and dirt and make-up, and it's 95 degrees with no wind, and you're on a beach surrounded by fire. By the end of the episode, you would have to go home and get scrubbed. But I love Hawaii. I will absolutely live there some day.'

He was having the time of his life on the show, featuring in 19 episodes in total – the longest job of his career thus far. And he was paid well too, between $20,000–$40,000 an episode. Yet it was to end all too soon for him. During some rare time off, he went on holiday in California's wine region to relax with his non-*Lost* friends, drink good wine and generally take a welcome break from the intensity of the set, but his tranquility was to be broken by a phone call informing him of some truly tragic news: Boone was to die in the next episode. '[It was] pretty devastating... Thank God I already had four glasses of really good Pinot in me,' said Ian.

The news seemed to come completely out of the blue for him as he was actually in the midst of searching for a permanent base in Hawaii: 'I almost bought a house there but, two days before I was going to fly back to look at one, I found out that my character was being killed off.'

He flew back to film and was less than thrilled about it: the death scene involved him falling off a cliff while inside a small aircraft which had crash-landed on the island sometime before their airplane had done the same. Boone sustains massive internal injuries from the fall, including a collapsed lung. Resident Island doctor Jack (played by Matthew Fox) attempts to save him by giving him a blood transfusion-by-sea urchin. If that sounds painful, Ian can definitely confirm that it was: 'I was spacey and nauseous and a little pissed,' he told *Entertainment Weekly*. 'It's hard walking a fine line between lucid and not lucid while Matthew Fox is ramming a needle into my chest.' It was, in his words, 'a long and exacerbating day simply because of the content and emotion, I'll be the first to say. Matt Fox and I (but especially him) went through the wringer that day. I couldn't wait to get it done but wanted to pay extremely close attention to the way in which that scene played out … We had a medical technician there to guide me in the right direction of how a human would react physically to those types of injuries; spanning from the collapsing of a lung to the moment of lucidity before someone dies. We got through but I think of it much.'

Boone's demise was in Ian's twentieth episode, called 'Do No Harm', which aired on 6 April 2005. His character's final words were 'Tell Shannon I…'

From the point of view of the *Lost* producers J.J. Abrams and Damon Lindelof – who had supported Ian so strongly in the beginning – it was absolutely necessary for Boone to die. Already they had almost killed several characters in the first season (Boone's sister Shannon among them), but they needed to give the show some gravitas and up the stakes by proving to the audience that no one was truly safe. 'It was a narrative imperative that we kill Boone,' executive producer Carlton Cuse told *Entertainment Weekly*. 'It sets in motion a chain of events leading to the season finale.' Boone's death enabled the conflict to develop between Jack and another character, Locke (played by Terry O'Quinn), which would be pivotal to the entire series.

Still, it was of little consolation to Ian, who felt as if he had been flung upside down on an emotional roller coaster. He was hurt but also grateful, sad but accepting, too – after all, on a show as new and experimental as *Lost* something had to give. He just didn't quite understand why it had to be him.

His character's death wasn't the end of his association with *Lost*, though. He appeared in 10 episodes after his death, coming back in Shannon's flashbacks over the course of a few episodes in Season Two and then he was back for the series finale in 2010.

He had to give credit to *Lost*, too – it had boosted his profile immensely. So much so that he discovered he had fans in some very strange places: 'I've got a lot of letters from prison. *Lost* was a big prison show but it's really crazy when you get the letter that says, "So, I'm getting out in three months, I've only been in for 17 years and I'd really like to meet you."' That must be pretty creepy for Ian!

In between appearances in Season One and the final Season Six, Ian didn't really watch the programme: 'When I left that show I needed to get on [with] my life. I wasn't going to just sit and watch every single episode that they were producing; it was very bittersweet. And now, going back, I haven't had time to watch five seasons of *Lost*. I wish I had, but it's just not the case. I know they're doing phenomenal work and what I have seen, it's like no other television show.' But that didn't mean to say he wasn't extremely grateful to have been a part of it, calling his year on the show the 'greatest experience of the greatest year of my life.' He was completely in awe of the work that J.J. Abrams and the rest of the *Lost* cast were doing – though understandably disappointed that he hadn't been able to be part of the magic for longer.

When he received the script for the finale, he was amazed: '[it] weighed about three pounds!' It was great fun for him to come back onto the show, albeit briefly, and he has great memories of his time on the beach: '[I loved] everything from being on a set with those phenomenally talented actors to watching rainstorms come, to looking at a 767 that's completely torn apart on this deserted beach in the middle of nowhere to being a part of one of the most amazing, historic television shows ever made. I wish I had stayed on the show, but it all works out the way it does. To be able to go back there and have that experience, with all of those people whom I've known for so long, and to have Damon Lindelof and Carlton Cuse still want me around, was a really, really cool experience.'

Chapter Four

Disaster Strikes

Stefan: That's the thing about Damon. He doesn't get mad – he just gets even. (1.06, 'Lost Girls')

For Ian, the future was now uncertain. It was 2005, and he felt on top of the world – despite being killed off on *Lost*, it was still the biggest show around and his profile had never been higher. 'It opened so many doors,' he admitted, 'but it definitely makes it harder to do any other show. It's like when you break up with someone and start dating someone else... you're always comparing the two.' He was prepared to get picky again and only audition for shows he really wanted.

Yet before he could even think about auditioning for any other roles, disaster struck his home state. Hurricane Katrina hit the Louisiana coastline on 29 August 2005. The Category 5 hurricane was the costliest natural disaster in US history, with 1,836 confirmed fatalities and damage caused to property estimated at $81 billion USD. 'I went back [home] 36 hours after the storm,' he remembered (most of his family were still living in Mandeville, Louisiana at the time). 'I couldn't get hold of my dad and I was freaked out. My whole family was fortunate – no one got hurt but my brother lost everything.'

After he'd finished helping his brother rebuild as much as he could, Ian got involved with fund-raising for the victims of Hurricane Katrina. He was a proud supporter of *Love Letters to the South*, a unique book full of photographic and written tributes from celebrities such as Johnny Depp, Justin Timberlake and Jon Bon Jovi, with a portion of the proceeds going to the American Red Cross and Habitat for Humanity; he even donated his own photograph and note. At the book launch, Ian explained what he had written: 'It was just a quick note to home with one of our favourite sayings down there: Laissez les bons temps rouler – let the good times roll. Which hopefully they will be rolling again soon down there.'

Even in the aftermath of the disaster, Ian still had to work. One of his first jobs post-*Lost* was in the movie *Pulse* (2006) with Kristen Bell and Christina Milian, which was filmed in the summer of 2005 in Romania. It was a remake of the Japanese horror film *Kairo* and Ian played Dexter, a computer hacker who realises that the previous owner of the machine he has recently purchased had stumbled upon a wireless signal that allowed spirits of the dead to travel to the world of the living. Even though this was a fairly flimsy horror-movie concept, it was a part that affected Ian quite deeply. He was always thinking about the role of electronics in our world, particularly our reliance on them and how that must be affecting our minds and bodies. '[*Pulse*] got me thinking about computers and electronics,' he told *People* magazine. 'We're made up of energy, so who's to say you can't transmit through electrical means? If you could transmit yourself wirelessly, then it's

Armageddon pretty much.' No one could accuse him of not being philosophical.

On its release *Pulse* was panned, with the website Rotten Tomatoes summing up critical opinion in one damning sentence: 'Another stale American remake of a successful Japanese horror film, *Pulse* bypasses the emotional substance of the original and overcompensates with pumped-up visuals and every known horror cliché.' It certainly didn't end up being the serious and noteworthy film that Ian had hoped to make.

After *Pulse*, Ian's acting résumé became a little sparse. He was still modelling, of course, and in early 2006 his agency DNA Models named him as one of their Top 10 Male Models. At the same time, he was also concentrating on real estate ventures and he bought himself a beautiful house in Malibu, where he could surf, take walks on the beach and generally get away from it all. 'I have a beach house in Malibu, so I'll go there, grab a surfboard or a sea kayak or whatever, and get outta here. The quality of life is so much higher any place you can ski in the morning and surf in the evening – there's something to be said for that.'

He also decided to try a different challenge: theatre. In October, 2005, Ian joined the cast of the Off-Broadway production *Dog Sees God: Confessions of a Teenage Blockhead*, written by Bert V. Royal, which re-imagined the characters from the 'Peanuts' comic strip as teenagers. It was a smart, subversive, unauthorised parody that generated shock laughs and had a real message about teenage conformity and homophobia. Ian starred as Matt (if you're familiar with the comic strips, then he played a grown-up Pigpen) alongside America Ferrera (*Ugly Betty*) and Eliza Dushku (*Buffy the Vampire Slayer*). He relished the challenge of live theatre, and although it was tough, he knew he had chosen a great role:

'The play is so cleverly written and it yields eight really great roles for young actors. Trip Cullman, our director, is the young theatre director to work with in NY. All of these elements including a magnificent cast are all the elements that will hopefully make this play great...' he wrote on his website. But it didn't help that he got really sick during the show's run: 'I was sick for 16 shows. Two straight weeks, I was deathly ill. And I ate a bag of Ricola [herbal cough drops from Switzerland] per show. ONE BAG.'

He was still exploring, too, and travelling, as getting to know other cultures and experience other ways of life was proving to be a real passion. It's what attracted him to the Hallmark-produced television movie *Marco Polo – The Discovery of the World* (2007), in which he was cast as the famous thirteenth-century Venetian explorer himself, who sets off on a landmark journey to China. The film was shot entirely on location in Hengdian World Studios in China, a five-hour drive from Shanghai and just two hours from Hangzhou (renowned as one of the most beautiful places in the world), where the real Marco Polo spent 17 years working for the Emperor Kublai Khan. Ian flew out to China and spent a few of the hottest months of the year there, from June to August of 2006. 'Places call you,' observed Ian to USA Today. 'Usually the Virgin Islands call people. China was calling me ... China is this place that had been closed off to Americans like forever. I remember as a kid growing up in the '80s you always heard, "Russia and China, you've got to be careful." Then you get there and there are these really peaceful people. Shanghai is one of my favourite cities. It blew my mind how beautiful this place is.'

The experience did almost kill him though! The temperatures soared past 38°C every day, and the cast ended up with severe sunburns and heat exhaustion. 'The humidity was worse than in India,' said Ian to Bend Weekly magazine. 'I lost 20 pounds in 8 weeks. I'd recommend going there in late spring, early fall, unless you want to lose some weight.'

As a backpacker and someone who loved adventure, Marco Polo's spirit really appealed to him: 'This guy of Anglo-Saxon descent walking through places like Afghanistan, it's a surprise that he didn't get killed in his first month. But the thing is, you always know what he did and what he saw, but you never know how he felt about it. He never talked about himself or his feelings, and he never judged anyone, which I think is pretty incredible.'

Ian was a gracious American in a foreign land, and he took the time to get to know some of his Asian colleagues – some of whom were working with an American film crew for the first time. One such actor, Kee Thuan Chye from Penang, Malaysia, played the role of chief mapmaker to Kublai Khan in the film. Kee's children (who were big *Lost* fans) were incredibly excited when they found out that their dad was getting to work with Ian. Kee spoke highly of Ian's generosity to *The Star* newspaper (a Malaysian English-language publication): 'I told Ian I couldn't go home without his autograph [for my children] and he was very pleased to write a personal and lengthy one for them.' It's these sorts of kind-hearted acts which demonstrate why Ian is held in such high regard in the acting world – Ian is no diva!

While he was getting to see more of the world, the world in turn was about to see a lot more of him. *Tell Me You Love Me* was an HBO drama that ran from September 2007 to July 2008, and revolved around three couples with intimacy issues. Variety described it as follows: '...makes *Sex and the City* look like a Saturday morning cartoon.' It must have been pretty steamy then! Ian was a guest star on six episodes, including one in which he gets completely naked. He described the show as: 'sexually graphic, but not gratuitous… It's definitely not what you want your girlfriend's parents watching.' Yet despite all the sexy scenes, the show never really found its audience and it was subsequently cancelled early into the second season.

Apart from a few other parts in TV movies such as *Lost City Raiders* and *The Tournament*, Ian's career appeared to be on a bit of a downward spiral. The problem was simple: he had gotten cocky. 'After *Lost*, I thought I was so cool. I had everything fucking totally thought out and together. And I said, "You know what? I wanna go do independent movies – I want to go to New York, I want to do theatre, I want to travel." And that's exactly what I did: I fell off the face of the fucking planet. I thought I was being cool and edgy, and it seemed like something Johnny Depp would have done fifteen years ago. Wrong. Biggest mistake. Except for the fact that I got to grow and be humbled and get my ass kicked,' he told *Nylon* magazine.

Of course what he needed was a part with bite to truly make his own. Suddenly, a vampire show came onto his radar with a choice role that he really, really wanted. But it wasn't *The Vampire Diaries*…

Chapter Five

Vampires Calling

Damon: It's not like we all hang out together at the vamp bar and grill. (1.11, 'Bloodlines')

Vampires had always held a special sway over Ian. For him, they weren't just a scary childhood bedtime story, though – his fascination with the undead continued well into adulthood. 'I was so obsessed with *The Lost Boys*,' said Ian. 'Really one of my favourite vampire movies is *Shadow of a Vampire* because it was just so not this romanticised, physical, sensual beautiful thing; it was really what I always imagined vampires to be. In that film, you almost feel like what it would be like to be cold and death.' It was also the actors playing the vampires who fascinated him: 'Willem Dafoe is on another planet as far as how talented he is.'

Being from New Orleans, of course, helped: 'There's a lot of vampire mystique and mythology that resonates [in New Orleans], and I was fascinated by it. I always wanted to play one.' His mother, Edna, used to keep an Anne Rice book by her bedside for a little night-time reading – vampire worship must run in the family!

And then along came HBO's *True Blood*, based on the Sookie Stackhouse series of novels by Charlaine Harris. It was a massive show with a big cast and an ambitious, racy script with a new take on the vampire myth: what if a blood substitute was created that enabled vampires to come out into the open? Would they be accepted into society? It looked set to be fun, sexy and a massive hit, with HBO throwing huge sums behind the show and into the marketing and publicity – even going as far as to sell the drink 'Tru Blood' in vending machines across the US. *True Blood* also had a cast of mostly little-known actors, with the exception of the female lead Sookie Stackhouse, who was played by Oscar-winning actress Anna Paquin (also well-known through her stints as Rogue in the *X-Men* trilogy). The principal male actors, Stephen Moyer (who played the main vampire, Bill Compton) and Ryan Kwanten (Jason Stackhouse) would go on to receive a massive boost to their profiles through appearing on the series. Clearly, if you wanted to be big, then you had to be on a vampire show.

Through his previous work on *Tell Me You Love Me*, Ian already had a good relationship with HBO and as soon as he read the script, he knew he wanted to be a part of it – but that didn't necessarily make him a shoe-in for the role.

Funnily enough, he wasn't even auditioning to play a vampire: he was after the role of Jason Stackhouse, the sexy-but-dimwitted brother of the feisty main character Sookie Stackhouse. 'I wanted to do *True Blood* so badly,' he told *TV Guide*. Unfortunately for Ian, the creators just didn't see him in the part. 'I just couldn't convince Alan Ball [creator of *True Blood*] that was my role. And then I didn't get it, and I was very bummed.' Eventually Ryan Kwanten was picked to play Jason.

'Bummed' seems like understatement for the way Ian felt about losing the role. Once again, he felt the cold shadow of failure creep up on him. The shows and movies he had taken part in since *Lost* had never really felt like the real deal and there were times when he thought he was never going to work again. 'It's really funny. As an actor, you always think that whatever job you have is going to be your last. In some way, shape or form, you think you're going to screw it up and you're never going to work again. And it literally took five years [after *Lost*] to find another show.'

After he was rejected from *True Blood*, Ian couldn't bring himself to watch the show. Naturally, he wanted as little to do with vampires as possible. So when his manager passed him yet another script for a series called *The Vampire Diaries* involving teenaged undead, he felt like running a mile. That was until he actually read the script. He was lying in bed with his then-girlfriend, 'she's reading Salinger, and I'm reading this script called *The Vampire Diaries*. And I thought, "You know what, man? This is gonna be the coolest character on television." There was no doubt about it.'

Ian soon realised this was the opportunity he had been waiting for: he instantly understood the character of Damon, the bad-boy vampire with killer charm. However, there was just one problem: he was nowhere near LA for the time the auditions were happening; he was actually in Las Vegas for a pizza convention. One of his many ventures outside of acting was investments – especially in real estate – which culminated in him owning one third of a gourmet pizza restaurant called McClain's Pizzeria in Sun Valley, Idaho, along with his sister and brother-in-law. But Ian wasn't about to give up because of a little distance. 'I desperately wanted [the part of Damon]. My girlfriend and I were in the desert in Vegas and I realised I'd missed this meeting. My agent called me back and said, "They need you there at 11 in the morning, having memorised nine pages of the script." It's now 9 o'clock at night in Vegas. We got up very early and I drove across the desert while she slept. I taped my pages together; that's how I worked on the material.'

In retrospect, it seems as if Ian's rush to get back caused him more harm than good for he well and truly fluffed the audition. And although he didn't know it at the time, he actually had the part in the bag without even having to turn up. The minute that Kevin Williamson, the creator of the show, heard Ian Somerhalder was interested in the part of Damon, he was sold. 'Ian comes vampire-ready,' he told *TV Guide*.

The fact then that Ian blew his audition made the process a little more difficult. After all, it was key in the eyes of the producers, the studio and the network that they should secure the perfect actor to play Damon. Meanwhile, Ian himself knew that it was a great part: 'It was a tough process getting this show because it was THE show to get. There was a lot of competition. Damon is one of the best characters you could ever dream of playing so I set my sights on him and made it happen.' It took those in charge of the production 10 days to finally sign off on him as Damon. 'Ten days of mental torture,' was how Ian described it.

Meanwhile, Kevin had a job to convince the network execs that Ian truly was Damon: 'To be honest, the first time [Ian] read for Damon, he didn't really bring it. Everyone said, "Oh, he's definitely got the look, he looks like Damon," but he just didn't bring it when he read. Still, I knew he had it in him. After talking to him, he said that this was really the exact role he'd been looking for. He wanted it so badly so at that point, for me, it was just about getting him the role, convincing the network to roll the dice with him. Ian was a gamble. We took a gamble on him, and he delivered.'

Later on, Ian explained to *Coup De Main* magazine why his audition had been such a disaster. It's clear that he let the nerves take over: 'If you, for some reason, get nervous, drink too much coffee, take too much B12, guess what? Your energy level skyrockets and you sort of get out of your rhythm and it's really heartbreaking to find something that you know in the deepest deep of your soul that you can play and you kind of blow it.' He later added, 'getting these roles for each and every one of us was extraordinarily horrible.'

But the torture was over – Ian had landed the part of Damon Salvatore. Damon was written up as a vampire without a conscience, who embraces his power over humankind. Manipulative, arrogant, remorseless and drop-dead sexy, he relishes being able to control, feed on and kill humans – the very antithesis to his brother, the broody Stefan.

In the television version of *The Vampire Diaries* (which differs from the novel and more about that on the Paul side), in the late eighteenth century, just after the American Civil War, Damon is turned into a vampire by the beautiful Katherine Pierce. He believes himself truly in love with Katherine, even though she is playing him off against his brother. The truth is revealed when Damon finds out that Katherine has turned both him and his brother into vampires, even though she promised it would just be him who would receive the 'privilege'.

Regardless of Katherine's betrayal, Damon still loves her. He believes that she was trapped beneath a church in Mystic Falls and that now, in the twenty-first century, finally the time has come to free her. Damon is driven halfway mad by his desire for Katherine and it fuels all his anger and frustration. Like his brother, he is intrigued by Elena's resemblance to Katherine and enjoys toying with his sibling, always threatening to move in on his girl. Of course the danger always looms that one day his threats might turn to reality and he might not be able to help himself.

For Ian, it was the perfect part. 'Damon is Dionysius,' he said, comparing his character to the Greek god of wine and ecstasy; 'he has an appetite for everything.' Now, all he had to do was figure out just how he was going to play a bloodthirsty, lustful 160-year-old vampire and make him believable. He knew he had a hard job ahead of him: 'It's a little strange. I actually don't like blood – it freaks me out a little bit. But when you think about being hungry, and you think about a time when you were stuck on a plane or you were somewhere without food, or you see people that are starving in the world and you think about how intense that is, and then you imagine being a vampire and having 160 years of life experience, and the knowledge of humanity, love, death and history, and on top of that your senses are heightened by 1,000 per cent, it's a very intense proposition. So, trying to inhabit someone who has that much knowledge of the world is a feat. I hope I'm doing it right and living it as truthfully as possible.'

And so he turned to some of his acting idols to inform him: 'I don't know of one specific actor, I just know that the ones who I've always been drawn to, that always amazed me whether they were good or bad – like Cary Grant, Jack Nicholson, Ed Harris – they all have something that was interesting. Whether they were being an antagonist or a protagonist, there's always something in their eyes. You could never quite tell what they were thinking, you just knew that they were thinking something and it probably wasn't good.'

The Cary Grant connection was to be a big factor in how Ian played Damon, as he explained to audiences at PaleyFest (the William S. Paley Television Festival dedicated to showcasing new and exciting media): 'There was a certain sense when you watched these men, when you watch a guy like Cary Grant on screen, you see the effortless fluidity with which he speaks and breathes and moves, and you go, "Ah, whoa!" They're just carefree and there's something about that that makes you want to watch every single frame.' He also took inspiration from former *Lost* cast-mate, Josh Holloway. Ian had always wanted to play Sawyer and this, in a way, was his chance so he called up Josh and said, 'Dude, I'm basing a lot of this character off of Sawyer – hope you don't mind?' Turned out, Josh didn't mind a bit.

Ian simply relished getting to play the bad guy for once. He told AOL TV: 'Damon is a bastard and I love playing him. I've spent my entire career brooding, so it's been great not to take myself too seriously. Damon's good fun – I would love to hang out with him.' It also helped that Damon was one of the best characters for Kevin Williamson to pen: 'I love writing for Damon. It's just about staying true to what Damon is, and Damon is a killer. He's driven by this love for Katherine that he's trying to get back, but at the core Damon is a killer. He's dark, and if anybody thinks he's going to suddenly soften up, they're going to be waiting a long time. He's a true predator and he needs to feed. Could the love of a woman possibly change him a little bit? Is there some humanity there? Maybe. Maybe, someday, but today is not that day. Don't hold your breath for that.'

Really, for Ian the beauty of this role was that it had a future – *The Vampire Diaries* just wouldn't be the same without him. And because he's already dead, the chances of him getting killed off are that much slimmer!

Chapter Six

Bloodbath

Alaric Saltzman: I think Stefan is a good guy. But at the end of the day, he's still a vampire. (1.18, 'Under Control')

Rewind a moment back to 2008 when vampires were the hottest Hollywood commodity: *Twilight* has smashed out of the box office and skyrocketed Robert Pattinson into demi-god status, deigning us mere mortals with his tousled hair and golden eyes. *True Blood*, a much more adult, darker and sexy take on the vampire myth, smoulders on the small screen, courtesy of HBO. Everyone was desperate to cash in on the vampire trend and it seemed there really couldn't possibly be any more room for vampires on our screens, small or large – or could there?

Even Ian admits to being at first incredibly sceptical despite being able to instantly tell how great a character Damon was. Indeed, he could totally see where the cynics were coming from. 'No – I mean, look, it was snicker-able,' Ian told *Vampire*

Diaries' Source. 'If you weren't a *Twilight* fan or you weren't into the vampire thing or you're oversaturated with *Twilight*, and you saw this show coming out on the CW, which is basically more vampires, like *Twilight*, but on television… if you're going to snicker, that's what you're going to snicker at. And there's an interesting thing that by virtue of this vampire oversaturation of the market, I think what people fail to realise is that within this vampire genre there's an immense amount of storytelling capability. There are a lot of great stories that come out of this; that's why it's so popular. So, to answer your question, was I surprised that people were snickering? No.'

Paul Wesley (cast as Damon's rival brother, Stefan Salvatore) had his doubts, too. 'There was some trepidation of, "Hmm, this could kind of go in a really cheesy direction and it could be riding the coat-tails of something,"' he remembers thinking when he first read the script.

Yet, believe it or not, no one was more sceptical than the creator of *The Vampire Diaries* himself, Kevin Williamson. 'In the beginning I didn't want to be involved with it, because I felt like sort of a *Twilight* rip-off, no matter what came first,' he told *The Torch Online*.

For him, there was also the little matter of that other vampire show: 'The second season of *True Blood* was all it took to make me not want to do vampires, because it was my favourite show and I wasn't about to jump into the fray.'

Still, he couldn't altogether dismiss *The Vampire Diaries*' proposal (thank goodness!). Williamson was on the hunt for a show… and had been for a long time. Having wrapped a short-lived television drama called *Hidden Palms* in July 2007, he was certain of just two things: first, that he wanted to do something completely different, and second, that he was keen to collaborate with his long-term friend Julie Plec. They just needed the right idea to get behind.

Kevin Williamson has built a career around writing for a teen audience and has a string of successful television shows and movies to his credit. Yet as a writer and director, he didn't have immediate success. Born on 14 March 1965 in New Bern, North Carolina, he spent years working on film sets – sometimes as an actor, sometimes as an assistant director – any odd job he could be hired to do in that kind of environment. Yet behind the scenes, he was unhappy and sensed his career was stalling. 'I was in a hard place, working as an assistant to someone here in Hollywood – a desk job, sort of in the wasteland of life,' he told the *New York Times*. 'I decided: I've got to do something. I'm got to figure out what I'm going to do with the rest of my life.'

Indeed, his unhappiness stemmed from high-school days when an English teacher ripped apart a short story he had written for an assignment: 'She didn't like me for some reason, I couldn't figure out why. When you're 15 or 16 you never know why the teacher is being mean to you,' he told the *New York Times*. That teacher went on to say some damning words that were to hang over him like a curse: 'She ripped [my story] up and said to me that I had a voice that shouldn't be heard.'

All that changed, though, when an idea sparked in his mind. It was 1994 and he was watching *Turning Point* – a TV series (also known in America as a newsmagazine) featuring hour-long programmes on a single 'real-life' topic, often of a sensational nature – like the O.J. Simpson trials or the Manson Family murders. This time, the episode was covering Danny Rolling, also known as 'The Gainesville Ripper': a serial killer who murdered five college students in Florida.

Morbidly fascinated, Williamson wondered what might happen if a group of teenagers, all well versed in the classic horror movie clichés, were pursued by a serial killer. Would they be able to thwart him or would they fall into the same traps?

Kevin knew he had struck a gold mine with this idea; he worked his regular job and came back home at night to write feverishly until the script was done. He remembers the anguish of those days, never sure if he was about to make his mark: 'I always wanted to direct – that's my passion. I was an actor. That went nowhere. I tried directing theatre. Nope. I wrote this movie called *Killing Mrs. Tingle*. Sold it. It sat on the shelf. My unemployment dried up. I couldn't get work. I had borrowed money from all my friends. So, I wrote *Scary Movie* [later re-titled *Scream*]. Just banged all it out, as fast as I could.'

Scream was picked up by Dimension Films and directed by infamous horror director Wes Craven (also responsible for terrifying audiences with *A Nightmare on Elm Street* and *The Hills Have Eyes*, among others). It came out in December 1996 to massive audiences and much acclaim, was credited with rebooting the slasher-film industry and launched Williamson as king of the teen horror genre. He followed up this success with two more *Scream* movies and *I Know What You Did Last Summer* (1997), cementing his position. Meanwhile, the fascination with the *Scream* franchise still hasn't died down and *Scream IV* came out on 15 April 2011.

The key to his success with *Scream* was the way he just understood teens. He spoke passionately about the respect he had for his young adult audience while writing the script: 'You know, teenagers are so savvy and smart,' he told *Film Radar* in 2002. 'VCRs and the Blockbuster generation had surfaced. They know these films like the back of their hands. What if they used their knowledge of these films and found themselves in the same situation, what would happen? I sort of started with that kernel of an idea and just ran with it. That's how it all came about.'

However, he wasn't about to be pigeonholed as a horror specialist: Williamson already had another project up his sleeve. In 1995 Paul Stupin, a producer for the Fox Network, approached Kevin to see if he had a teen-oriented television series in him – they had just bought *Beverly Hills 90210* (the original) and were looking for something similar. It turns out that Kevin did have something ready: a story about a group of high-schoolers growing up in a small town that pretty much mirrored his own upbringing. '*Some Kind of Wonderful* meets *Pump Up the Volume*, meets *James at 15*, meets *My So-Called Life*, meets *Little House on the Prairie*,' was how he pitched it. Ultimately, Fox passed on the show but another network – The WB – were also on the hunt for a new show and gave him the go-ahead. Thus, on 20 January 1998, *Dawson's Creek* was born.

The series was to be a landmark in television produced for teens. Apart from launching the careers of several young actors and actresses – Katie Holmes, Joshua Jackson, Michelle Williams and James Van Der Beek (to name a few) – it redefined how teenagers could be portrayed on screen. The show's trademark was its sophisticated language combined with its smart, open approach to the complex, real-life crises facing teens in their day-to-day lives.

Dawson's Creek had a love-it or hate-it premiere! Some critics saw it as brilliant (an 'addictive drama with considerable heart,' said *Variety*) while others thought it vacuous and too risqué ('I can't get past the consuming preoccupation with sex, sex, sex,' said the *Cincinnati Inquirer*). Regardless of the critics' opinion, teens totally got the show and they loved it. It became the defining television series for The WB (which later became The CW) and firmly established Williamson as the go-to writer for smart, sexy teen dramas.

Of course that doesn't mean that everything he turned his attention to turned to gold. When you produce something as successful as *Dawson's Creek*, often it's hard to follow up straight away with equal brilliance. Williamson was always going to be judged by the success of that one show. His next small-screen endeavours included *Wasteland* (1999), which was about a group of struggling twenty-something actors in New York. 'I think it's maybe a victim of expectations,' said the show's director Steve Miner after it premiered to lukewarm reviews and ratings. *Wasteland* represented Williamson's first attempt to break away from the teenage voice. 'I don't think of myself as the voice of the teenage era and I never have,' he told *Entertainment Weekly*, back in 1999 before he had embraced the fact that actually, he is! 'I'm growing up as a writer and I hope adults will accept *Wasteland* because my goal is to appeal to that late 20s to early 30s age range.'

When *Wasteland* wasn't the success he had intended it to be, Williamson moved on to *Glory Days* (2002), which was also known as *Demontown* and not to be confused with *Glory Daze*, the 80s-set college fraternity comedy. It had a horror/mystery feel to it, and only ran for two months. The premise was about a successful novelist whose bestselling novel was based on people from his small hometown. When he returns to try and overcome severe writer's block, the townspeople are none too happy to have him back and mysterious, unexplained events begin to happen around him. Despite a relatively strong viewership at the start, interest quickly waned and the show was subsequently axed. Another television venture was called

Hidden Palms, again involving a murder-mystery, this time set in sunny Palm Springs. After its initial eight-episode run, it too was cancelled. Meanwhile, Williamson didn't fare much better on the big screen, with follow-up movies to *Scream* including *Venom*, *Cursed* and his first-ever directorial debut, *Teaching Mrs. Tingle* (1999) – the payback script for that English teacher who once eviscerated his writing. In fact, he had to rename his original script, *Killing Mrs. Tingle*, after a string of high-profile real-life high school murders made it inappropriate and even then it absolutely tanked at the box office.

No, what Williamson needed was this new project called *The Vampire Diaries* – and thank goodness he had his collaborator Julie Plec on hand to persuade him not to get distracted by the *Twilight* connection and to keep on reading.

Plec and Williamson's working relationship goes all the way back to *Scream*. 'I was [director] Wes [Craven's] assistant on *Scream*,' Plec recalls. 'It was [Kevin's] first movie that ever got made, my first movie. I was 22, just out of college. We were two kids in a candy store, up in Santa Rosa, California, on location, making a movie.'

Plec moved to Los Angeles almost as soon as she was able. She always knew that she wanted to work in the movie industry and never had a plan B. 'I think that's why I survived,' she admits. 'If I had a Plan B, I might not have stuck with it through the bad times as long as I did.'

Her first job was as 'the second assistant to an agent named Susan Smith,' she told NiceGirlsTV, but she quickly realised that being an agent wasn't for her. It didn't involve enough creativity and so she only lasted in the job for three months. Then a friend told her about an exciting opportunity to work for the notorious horror-movie director Wes Craven, as his assistant. She took the job and it was to change her life forever

– she was even the one who managed to convince Wes to direct the fun, modern horror movie written by a nobody in the industry called *Scream*. It was like fate. All of a sudden, Plec found herself working with 'every young hot star of the moment and a crew that became my LA family.' Most importantly, she met and instantly connected with the young writer of the film, one Kevin Williamson.

The two became firm friends. 'We used to sit up on night shoots [during *Scream*] and sing Kenny Rogers' songs and talk about our future,' she said. It was this friendship that was to become one of the defining threads in the fabric of her career. She would collaborate with Kevin on other projects – mostly movies like *Teaching Mrs. Tingle* and *Cursed* (their werewolf project) – while she worked on her own shows. Yet her career-defining show pre-*The Vampire Diaries* was without Williamson: a teen television drama called *Kyle XY* (2006–09). It was the first time she really got to showcase her writing skills and worked on building a show from the ground up.

Kyle XY was about a young boy who is found in the middle of a forest with no memory of life before that moment and strangest of all, no sign of a belly button. He is adopted into the Trager family and gradually discovers that he has extraordinary powers. When the show debuted on 26 June 2006, it was to lots of hype and solid reviews, but ratings steadily declined throughout the running time and it was eventually cancelled. The last episode aired on 16 March 2009, with many plot lines left unresolved. It meant that Plec and the rest of the *Kyle XY* team didn't get to close out the show and wrap up the storylines as intended: 'If I had any control over how and when *Kyle XY* ended, things would have been handled differently but I, like all of us involved with the show, had to stop when we were told to stop. It was disappointing, knowing that we couldn't deliver a final chapter to our story,' she admitted.

A special segment on the DVD called '*Kyle XY*: Future Revealed' was included, in which the writers and producers talked about how they would have resolved matters, given the opportunity. Plec remembers the show with fondness: 'I loved working on that show and the friends I made with the other writers, actors and producers are some of my strongest friendships still.'

Once *Kyle XY* had ended, she was at a loose end: she wanted another show, but she wasn't sure what. She had been following the vampire trend – she was a die-hard fan of *Twilight* – and has a history of being drawn to the supernatural but then someone at The CW passed her a series of novels...

Just like the novels (read more about them on the Paul side), the idea for *The Vampire Diaries*' show didn't come from its creators, but from the network – The CW. The CW ('C' from CBS and 'W' from Warner Brothers, the two parent companies) was a relatively new network at that time, an amalgamation of TV channels UPN and The WB. UPN had aired shows such as *America's Next Top Model* and *Everybody Hates Chris*, whereas The WB had hits like *Dawson's Creek*, *Smallville* and *Supernatural*. Together, they had a mission to focus 'intently on finding shows that would finally define The CW as a net for young people, especially younger women.' (*Variety*). One of The CW's first hits was with *Gossip Girl* (2007–), a connection that would lead to the network securing its biggest property yet.

The CW had bought the television option to *The Vampire Diaries*' series in conjunction with Alloy Entertainment (who produced the novels) and were looking for the right writer/director/producers to bring the story to life on the small-screen. They told Plec: 'We have a property that we've been dying to do. We absolutely want to do a vampire show, and we'd love for you to look at it.' They wanted a vampire story as they hoped that the paranormal romance would prove the perfect complement to their already successful show, *Supernatural*.

Plec read the books first, and loved them. She told Williamson to, 'Keep reading, keep reading!' even when he felt inclined to stop. It was only once he had delved deeper into the series that Kevin realised the true potential of *The Vampire Diaries*: this wasn't to be seen as simply a rip-off of *Twilight* because it was about more than just two young people in love. Of course, it was about two young people in love (and that was important), but also about the effect of vampires on a small-town community that has its own deep, dark history. Williamson admitted that a light bulb went off in his head when he realised: 'this is [much more] than a story about a small town... [it's] about the underbelly of a small town, and what lurks under the surface.'

'I had to make myself believe that so that I could move forward and I talked myself into it, because I thought, "If I can just get past the pilot, which is *Twilight* – girl meets guy in school – and if I can get past that, I bet there's a show here that I can add something to,' he told the audience at PaleyFest. Between them, the two writers were up-to-date on all the latest vampire hits, with Plec being a huge *Twilight* fan and Williamson never missing an episode of *True Blood*.

Of course, neither begrudges the influence of *Twilight* and they are, in fact, 'happy to ride the coat-tails.' Much of the initial interest in and buzz surrounding the show comes from having a built-in, vampire-ready audience.

Still, there was no way the show would have survived had it not been able to differentiate from the sparkling vampires and prove itself a hit in its own right. For that, Kevin Williamson believed, they just needed to get audiences past the *Twilight*-esque pilot.

Chapter Seven

Pilot Takes Flight

Elena: I would say drop dead, but... (1.20, 'Blood Brothers')

On 30 March 2009 Ian flew to Vancouver, Canada, along with the two other leads: Paul Wesley (who was to play his brother, Stefan Salvatore) and Nina Dobrev (cast as the innocent young girl in the middle, Elena – and her doppelgänger Katherine). They were heading up to Hollywood North to begin shooting the pilot episode of *The Vampire Diaries*. For those unfamiliar with the term, a 'pilot episode' is the first-ever episode of a series and it's often the test to see whether an entire series will be successful. Networks frequently axe a whole series based on the performance of the pilot and as a result most producers won't splash out on fancy, expensive permanent sets just for one episode. Often this means that pilots are not a true reflection of the series to come.

And that was certainly true of *The Vampire Diaries*. Although the show is set in a fictional town in the state of Virginia, co-creators Kevin Williamson and Julie Plec chose to shoot the pilot in Vancouver for the incentives. Plenty of The CW's television shows have their permanent homes in Vancouver so there were ready-made sets available for *The Vampire Diaries'* use. For example, the show used Templeton Secondary School for Mystic Falls High – the same school featured in *Smallville, Kyle XY* and *Supernatural.*

For the director of the pilot and supervising producer, the team had Marcos Siega on board – an inspired decision. 'We're so lucky because we have Marcos Siega, our supervising producer,' Kevin told the *LA Times*. 'He directs about every third episode, and he's really responsible for the look of the show and the tone. He's out there making sure that the quality stays up to our standard. We don't have a big budget, but I think we really stand up to other shows with a much larger budget, and that's because of Marcos. Give him a light bulb and he can make anything look good.'

Siega made his name directing music videos for huge teenage rock bands such as Blink 182, All American Rejects and Weezer. Later he graduated from videos to television and directed several episodes of that other vampire show, *True Blood*, along with other popular shows like *Dexter*. He knew the quality of writing that went into a hit show, and he recognised that *The Vampire Diaries* had it. The wit and sharpness of Williamson and Plec's script shone through. One script reviewer called *The Vampire Diaries'* pilot episode, 'quick, witty and hilarious; I love how the script describes its characters and certain situations. Two characters in the beginning of the pilot script are described as "Arren, 24, has that cute-I'm-probably-gonna-die-soon-look" and "Brooke, 24, pretty, smart-faced. Has that I'll-probably-live-longer-than-my-boyfriend-look." Are you serious??? Yes they are.' (Vampire Nerd).

And Siega already had an enthusiast for his work in Nina Dobrev (who plays Elena): she was a massive fan of *True Blood*. 'I'm obsessed with it,' she admitted. 'I got to meet the entire cast at Comic-Con [the comic book and popular arts convention] and hang out with them, and that was awesome. I basically died and went to heaven. Michael [McMillian], the guy who plays the preacher [Steve Newland], we talked for a long time, and we had the same agent, so that was the start of our conversation. [The *True Blood* cast] were so cool, we ended up talking and hanging out for a lot of the night at the EW party. And because of that, we really got to know each other, a lot of us. I know obviously because we all have vampire themes in our shows, we're going to be constantly running into each other and now we know each other. It's kind of fun.'

She acknowledges that having Marcos Siega on board, and later, another *True Blood* director John Dahl, added extra 'edge' to *The Vampire Diaries*: 'We're trying to make it a little more cinematic than you usually see on The CW – a little edgier, a little darker. We're trying to push the envelope as much as we possibly can for network television.' They couldn't go quite so far as *True Blood* (no nudity, for example) but they could still push the barriers in other ways, building tension and intensity into the script without using full-blown sex.

Another benefit of having some *True Blood* presence on-set was that Siega could point out if they were sometimes getting a little too close for comfort. As Williamson pointed out, it was difficult not to broach some of the same topics as *True Blood*: 'There are obvious similarities and obvious connections there. For example, vampires don't age. There was a *True Blood* episode this season where Sookie was concerned about that and of course, it's going to come up for Elena as well. When she's forty, Stefan will still look seventeen. Things like that are universal in the vampire mythology. We know this isn't a new story, a human woman falling in love with a vampire, so we just do our best to tell the classic stories with our own twist. Ultimately, we're going to go where our story takes us.' At one point, though, Siega refused to direct an episode that reminded him too much of *True Blood* and he managed to convince the writers to change the script. After all, they didn't want to get accused of vampire plagiarism!

So they had a touch of *True Blood* influence, but what about the teen vampire books and movies that kick-started the whole trend, *Twilight*?

Of all the cast members, Nina Dobrev was the biggest *Twilight* fan. 'I read the *Twilight* books before the movie and the whole craze happened,' she told *Entertainment Weekly*. 'And then I loved it. I was in love with Edward before every other girl that says she's in love with him was. Because I read them a long time ago shooting a movie in Salt Lake City, and one of Stephenie Meyer's friends said, "Make sure you read my friend's book." And I read it, and I was like, "This is actually really great." And then it turned into what it is now.'

According to Kevin Williamson, she also points out if he and his co-writer ever get too close to the *Twilight* format: 'Sometimes we'll write dialogue and Nina Dobrev (Elena) will say, "You do realise that's exactly what was said in *Twilight*, right?" And I'll tell her, "No, I had no idea."' They also like to poke a little fun at the connection, with Damon asking a female character in the show why a vampire sparkled.

Funnily enough, Ian Somerhalder and Paul Wesley weren't the only vampire kids on the Vancouver block at that time. 'When we were shooting the pilot for *The Vampire Diaries*, Kellan [Lutz] was filming *The Twilight Saga: New Moon* in Vancouver as well,' said Paul. 'And so they were all staying at the same hotel. We actually ended up hanging out a bunch of times. I was kind of like, this is either really lame or really cool that we're all hanging out. I was like, what is this? Like some sort of vampire gathering where we trade secrets?'

Naturally having the hottest teen vampires in the same place set the media pack into a frenzy and when Paul was spotted at a basketball game with female-vamp Ashley Greene (Alice in the *Twilight Saga* movies) it sparked a steady rush of rumours of some inter-vampire dating. Regardless of whether there were any romantic sparks, the two casts really hit it off. And it seemed some of the *Twilight* magic rubbed off on the cast too because when the pilot was screened at conventions all over America it was a huge success with the fans.

It was a tense moment for Kevin Williamson and Julie Plec as they were already well aware that the pilot wasn't even close to the strongest episode of their series: it was more of a 'setting the scene' episode and the one that bore the closest resemblance to their rivals. 'The pilot was very tough because it does have a lot of similarities to *Twilight* and there's no way around it,' Kevin told CanMag. 'We had to introduce – we had the story as he comes to town, the first day of school. That is the book. So we sort of are telling it in sort of that fashion, but we're switching things around. Once we get into it and we can establish all the characters, which is what – you know, the pilot, we had 10 characters to get out in 42 minutes. It's tough. And so now we can sort of sit back and start telling stories on a weekly basis. Then it all changes. That's when you'll see the differences, because you're watching a weekly show. We're not a movie with a beginning, middle, and end. We're actually evolving, and we get to evolve and just tell the stories, and it just sort of unrolls.'

The pilot was previewed at the 2009 San Diego Comic-

Con, one of the biggest comic book, science-fiction/fantasy and film/television conferences in the world. Critics, however, were understandably divided. Already wilting under vampire-fatigue and more ready with cynicism than a regular audience, most were quick to write off the pilot as a *Twilight* rip-off, plain and simple. 'I'm sure this show will have its audience, but boy am I not among them,' wrote Futon Critic. 'The final product proves to be just as predictable and cliché-filled as we expected. All in all, *Diaries* at best plays like a 44-minute music video for a much more interesting show and at worst a lifeless clone of things we've seen done before, and done much better.'

'Well, it stands to reason that this show will benefit from the vamp-craze sweeping the nation, but it still can't help but feel stale and derivative. Yes, despite the fact that it came first… food court goth at best,' quipped IGN. And, as might be expected, the hardcore sci-fi website io9.com had nothing good to say about it: 'Seriously, it's like *Dawson's Creek* without the witty banter and with vampires, so maybe *One Tree Hill* with vampires.'

But some critics could see past the pilot's flaws and to the potential of the show that lay beyond. *Blast* magazine wrote: 'Overall, the pilot for *The Vampire Diaries* is a great start for the series. Audiences will love the hints of humor thrown into the mix of drama, Somerhalder's delicious bad-boy taunts and the formulaic love story. Dobrev and Wesley are refreshing as their chemistry onscreen intensifies with each added scene. The only stark contrast is the narration of the diary entries, which comes across as awkward at times. The atmosphere for the series is balanced and the collaboration between talent and production are not over-the-top. There is a focus on keeping up the suspense until the final scenes.'

Meanwhile, thevampirediaries.net – whose audience adore the original L.J. Smith books and wanted to know how the series compared – was full of praise: 'What I feel comfortable saying, because I can only speak for myself, is that I'm really liking what I'm hearing from the producers about their overall vision. There's definite potential here and I think the show can easily strike a balance between its core love story and supernatural happenings now that it has the time to develop and twist and raise the stakes.'

With this kind of show, though, critical opinion is only a small part of the equation. The network had seen enough to know that it had something big on its hands yet the biggest test was still to come: would anyone actually tune in to watch?

Premiere day, aka D-Day, was set for 10 September 2009. Let's remember that *The Vampire Diaries* was originally commissioned as a lead-in to The CW's other hit show, *Supernatural* (2005–), and so the pilot was given the 8pm slot before the fifth season of *Supernatural* was to air at 9. But *The Vampire Diaries* blew *Supernatural* out of the water: it became the most-watched premiere in The CW's three-year history, with 4.9 million viewers tuning in across the States and another 1.5 million-strong audience in Canada. Combined with the DVR (i.e. pre-recorded) viewings, this figure jumped to 5.7 million. And so it was official – The CW had a hit on its hands.

Chapter Eight

The Next Stage

Damon: Do you know how liberating it is not having a master plan? Because I can do whatever the hell I want. (1.15, 'A Few Good Men')

Immediately the network gave Williamson and Plec the go ahead to commission more episodes and this gave them the confidence to search for a permanent set. In the end, they settled on Atlanta, Georgia – the biggest reason being because the city was offering some great tax incentives for film-makers!

It made for a huge change for the stars – especially for Nina Dobrev, who had only just moved out to LA, but it was loads of fun at the same time as it was the best bonding experience a cast could ask for. 'We all moved together and [started] hanging out and we feel like we really have a life here,' said Nina. She rented an apartment with Kayla Ewell, the actress who appeared as doomed Vicki Donovan, and then later with Sarah Canning (who plays her aunt, Jenna Sommers).

Being in Atlanta isolated them a little from *The Vampire*

Diaries' frenzy sweeping across the nation. After shooting the pilot, Paul Wesley, Ian and Nina went through a huge roll-call of photo shoots for promotions. Nina remembers the difficulty they all went through, trying to get the main promo shot – where she is lying on the ground on her back, flanked by the two brothers. 'We shot that on a green screen and I was in such an uncomfortable position, but it turned out really cool,' she said. The cast didn't really get to experience the finished product, however. Paul had friends calling him up from New York and Los Angeles (where one mall in particular, the Century City Mall in Los Angeles, was almost wallpapered with *The Vampire Diaries'* posters). 'We're a bit detached from it all down here in Georgia,' he admitted.

But they wouldn't be out on a limb for long: the producers geared up the cast to go on the convention circuit – apart from promoting the new show at Comic-Con, they hit up PaleyFest, Eyecon and many others. It was then that the cast truly got to discover what a hit they had on their hands and really started to connect with their fan-base. 'Our fans, they are awesome,' said Ian Somerhalder. 'You get to experience that enthusiasm at a decibel level that is second to none; they are so loud and amazing. I swear, it was the closest to being a Beatle I'll ever get.' Sometimes the screaming was so loud, the cast couldn't hear each other. 'Your eardrum vibrates and everything becomes like white noise in your ear,' he continued. 'You could scream and not hear yourself. You can hear the vibration coming out of your throat but you can't hear your own voice. Most people don't go to work when that happens. And I say that in all humility: I'm the luckiest dude I know.'

The change in location also had an impact on the weather in the series. As they shot the pilot in Vancouver at the end of March/April 2009, the cast were all in sweaters, jeans and jackets to fight the chill in the air but by the time they moved to sunny Atlanta, Georgia, to shoot episode two, it was boiling hot! At first they still had to keep their sweaters and leather jackets on for consistency before they could shed them for more appropriate clothing.

Williamson and Plec also made several cuts after watching the pilot and decided certain elements of the show just weren't working. One was the shape-shifting ability of the vampires – for example, in the books Damon can shift into a crow. They did make a nod to this in the pilot episode (you may notice a crow appearing in most of the scenes before Damon arrives), but the actual transformation was never shown. As the show went on, they phased the crow out almost entirely. It didn't help that, as Paul said in a PaleyFest panel, 'birds are uncooperative' to work with on a TV set. Julie also joked that they once had to wait 37 minutes for a crow to caw for a scene! It was too much, too soon, and they believed the crow (or more specifically, the shape-shifting) felt 'too supernatural' for the show!

Other elements phased out were the fog machine and the narrated diary entries. The pilot seemed to use the most rolling fog in a television show in recent memory (plus, having the vampires control the weather/fog felt almost overly powerful for the beginning of the show), and both it and the diaries came off as a bit too cheesy. That being said, Julie Plec noted on the VRO radio show that she and Kevin fought all the time about the journal entries – as she loved them but he didn't want them any more! 'We keep the idea of journalling alive in our mythology,' she said and after all, the show is called *The Vampire Diaries*!

As we have seen, when *The Vampire Diaries* premiered on television on 10 September 2009, it was to record ratings. The fact that Kevin Williamson considered the pilot to be the weakest episode seemed to have little bearing on its popularity, although it gave him the confidence to know that if audiences stayed captivated until further into the season, they'd be hooked for life. And it seemed like he was right: ratings continued to stay high even as the series continued – a sign this wasn't just a one-hit wonder. The show also went on to win the 2010 People's Choice Award for Favorite New TV Drama – proof once again that it had secured the love of the fans.

For the cast, the show seemed to be getting better and better, too. Ian's favourite episode was the same as Nina Dobrev's – episode five: 'The Lost Girls'. 'It's the one where Damon turns Vicki,' said Somerhalder to the *LA Times*. 'It's still my favourite. I read it, and I called Kevin [Williamson] and Julie [Plec, co-creators] to thank them. Me and Kayla Ewell [who played Vicki] had so much fun shooting that episode. It was before Kayla was gone. Her leaving really put a damper on the show for me, but when we shot that episode, it was innocent and it was happy. We didn't know anyone was dying. We all thought we were safe. We were just having a blast with the beautiful, tight script.'

And he was well positioned to comfort Kayla, as he knew exactly what it was like to be written out of a hot new show. In a way, it was worse for the actress as she knew it was coming, but couldn't help but bond with the cast anyway: 'I knew very early on,' she told *Entertainment Weekly*, 'but knowing it and actually going through it are two completely different things. Seven episodes is a lot of time to bond with people. Being back in LA has been harder than I thought it would be because this job was more special to me than any other job I've ever done.'

Like Boone Carlyle's death in *Lost*, Vicki's enabled a main character to make an emotional transformation – this time, it was Elena's brother, Jeremy. 'Funny story: In the original script,

Jeremy kills Vicki,' continued Kayla. 'And that's what we shot. Jeremy is forced to choose between saving the love of his life or his sister, and he chooses his sister. We shot the whole thing and I [moved back to] LA. Then about a week-and-a-half later, I got an e-mail from Kevin and Julie Plec asking me to come back to Atlanta to reshoot my death scene – only this time Stefan kills me. They chose to have Stefan kill me because it makes him more of a hero since he saves Elena. There was also the question of would Jeremy know to actually stake a vampire in the heart?'

So, what was the secret to *The Vampire Diaries'* almost-overnight success? It seemed like everything was coming together for the show: a great cast, an enthusiastic built-in fan-base, and network support, but *The Vampire Diaries* also handed Kevin Williamson the perfect mixture of success: part *Dawson's Creek*, part *Scream* – it was as if the show had been built for him. Yet he wasn't about to let it become a *Dawson's Creek* reboot – after all, this was the noughties and times had changed: 'The '90s were all about post-modern hip. It was the era of the self-aware teenager, but now it's just commonplace so to have all that self-aware dialogue seems trite. We've evolved out of it,' he told *Nylon* magazine. 'We're also a country at war. That's why the genre element of it all is so appealing. It's not real. It's a fantasy world. But teenager love stories are always so life and death. So what better place to tell a vampire story than in a story of life and death every week? I don't know why, but the vampire craze is really quite big. Julie loves *Twilight*. I love *True Blood*. And when we put [the way we work] together, what we get works well.'

That's not to say that he couldn't see the connection: 'I always said that the teenage years are just one big horror movie. High school is a horror movie.' And he was back writing for the audience he loved: 'That's why I write about teenagers. One of the things I learned while I was doing *Wasteland* is that writing about people in their twenties – who cares? It's just a big "who cares?" Nothing's life or death then. When you're 25, who cares if a love doesn't work out? You will find another one. But when you're 16, it's life and death. As I've discovered, it's that way when you get older too. There's your first love and your last love. Those are the epic moments. Everything else is just in between.'

Chapter Nine

Being Damon

Damon: Have fun with the Mystic Queen...
I know I did. (1.21, 'Miss Mystic Falls')

Ian was ready to throw himself full force into the character of Damon. And luckily, given the show's format, he has plenty of opportunity to vary his performance. Already he gets to mix up modern with old-fashioned as the show flashbacks to the eighteenth century when Damon and Stefan were first turned by the evil Katherine, and he hopes there will be other opportunities to get dressed up in period costume: 'There are always decades that interest people. For me, that's the Roaring Twenties. I'd love to see Damon in the '20s. The '30s, the '40s... oh God, the '70s! Could you imagine Damon wearing a polyester shirt, just this huge lapel and really fluffy, long hair? Oh man!'

The truth is, no fan really wants to see Damon in a polyester shirt – they'd much rather see him in no shirt at all! 'I ask and beg, and call Julie [Plec] and Kevin [Williamson] all the time, "Can I please get naked?"' joked Ian at PaleyFest. Costume designer Jennifer Bryan spoke to *Entertainment Weekly* about how the 'shirtless' scenes are decided: 'There's a couple of ways that it has evolved. I would say almost all the time, the writers put it in but they dole it out in small measures. If the story calls for it, that's what happens but I don't think they had expected such a strong positive reaction, like, "More! More!"' How could they not expect it with such hotties as Ian and Paul at the helm?

The amount of fun Ian was having playing Damon was really put into perspective when he was called back to the *Lost* set to film the series finale, which aired on 23 May, 2010. There was no love lost between him and his former character, Boone Carlyle; he didn't miss playing him at all.

'Poor Boone, I just think the guy found himself out of his element. He was thrown into a really iffy situation, but Damon is so fun. Boone was at a tough point in his life, at that point, and Damon – I have so much fun playing this role, and to go from Boone – heavy-headed, heartbroken, "I just slept with my sister" Boone – to Damon, it was a really funny transition, and that transition all happened within one twenty-four-hour period. I literally left Hawaii, left set, flew to Atlanta, landed and went to set.' He did appreciate, however, how the writers of *Lost* had managed to tie up the immensely complex plot: 'The finale was such a monumental thing because it spanned six years of phenomenal storytelling,' Ian told AOL. 'For some viewers it was exuberant because it answered the questions they wanted answering and it was somewhat disappointing for other viewers. We all had an idea of where we wanted the story to go and it ended, I think, very powerfully, very neatly, and yet like any good story it still left you answering questions.'

Of course, he knows there's a huge disparity in levels of

success between *Lost* and *The Vampire Diaries*: 'What's crazy is, here's the difference. When I was in Hawaii shooting *Lost*, I was in Jack Bender's office – he's the directing executive producer – I looked up on his wall and there are all these big newspaper clippings and it says, "*Lost* Season Two Premiere" or whatever, and there are 31 million viewers in the States. This show [*The Vampire Diaries*] has five [million viewers], so it's significantly less, but it's the power of the youth culture, and that's what's so amazing.

'Like the fact that *The Vampire Diaries* won the People's Choice Award – it's a numbers game. The people vote. And crazy enough, they voted for our show. It's a really active audience, and that's the other thing. They're active online, and this network [The CW] – they're geniuses at online network marketing – and it's so interactive now. We know that this is such a great way to talk with fans. It's insane. You can push a button and a hundred thousand people will get that instantly.' Of course, in the last instance Ian was referring to the power of Twitter, of which you can read more about a little later on.

There was also the small matter of Ian getting to return to the set of *Lost* as a bona fide star himself – in fact, he was now the key anchor of a hit show, which put his *Lost* experience into perspective. It also meant that for once, the *Lost* stars were the ones who became star-struck! OK, well maybe not the stars themselves, but certainly their children. Matthew Fox's (Jack on *Lost*) 12-year-old daughter was so distraught when Damon killed Stefan's best friend Lexi that Matthew had to set up a talk between the two. Ian described the incident to *TV Guide*: 'It's 1:30 in the morning – there's a six-hour time difference between Hawaii and Atlanta – and Matthew calls me and says, "Listen, dude, she wants to talk to you. You need to justify some things to her. She's not happy with you." So she drilled me with these questions and I was explaining my actions and saying, "There are times when you find yourself in situations that you may have to hurt someone for the betterment of the family, which is what Damon was doing." And every time I'd start explaining something, she'd go "Yep, uh huh. And...?" It was an interesting hour for me!'

When it came to his character's fascination with Nina's character Elena, at first Ian had trouble figuring out what a vampire aged 160 years plus would want out of a teenage girl, let alone why he would want to suffer going back to high school – an experience Ian himself would not want to repeat. How would he relate to her? What would he find interesting about her? 'It's interesting, if you think about it. If you were connecting to a ten-year-old on a real basic [non-sexual] human level, it's interesting. We spend our lives in search of knowledge and money, and history and art and music, and film and food and travel. Damon has so much of that, and I think what's kind of interesting and amazing is, when he really is standing there, talking to Elena, who's seventeen years old, he finds there's a commonality; there are common denominators there that are unexplained. There's a little mystery. It doesn't matter. My niece is a year-and-a-half old. The time that I have with her is my most cherished time on the planet, literally. You're sitting there with this giant person, who's this big [his hands depict someone tiny], who blows your mind, everything they do and say – and you connect with that child. And she's thirty years younger than I am,' he told *StarPulse*.

Ian is extremely comfortable in his own skin, but if there was any one trait that he could steal from Damon, it would be his mind control: 'The mind-compulsion thing is pretty cool. He can literally look at people in their eyes and then make them do whatever he wants; that could be really dangerous. He can also get into people's minds and move at the speed of light. Being able to read someone's mind and get inside of their head could be really dangerous. He can also make them see what he wants them to see.' Ooh, creepy!

For Ian, it's always the fans that keep him going. His *The Vampire Diaries'* followers are, of course, much younger than the fans he was used to on *Lost*, 'which makes it really adorable. Every 13-year-old girl in America who's not watching *Lost* is watching this show, and they're so cute and so into it. They have so many questions and they get so excited; I just want to hug them. The little girls get scared because they think I'm a vampire and that I'm going to kill them!'

Luckily, Ian isn't the murderous type! He just plays the role with such superb confidence and ease that his fans might be forgiven for forgetting where Ian ends and Damon begins.

Chapter Ten

Behind the Scenes

Damon: I'm not a hero, Elena. I don't do 'good' – it's not in me. (1.22 'Founder's Day')

On the set of *The Vampire Diaries* the atmosphere is electric. The entire cast is young and attractive, and perhaps owing to the fact that they have had to move out to Atlanta, Georgia, together, in relative isolation from the Hollywood scene, they've had the opportunity to bond more than most other casts. Ian joked to the *LA Times*, 'Well, we'd better love each other, because we're stuck with each other for 185 days a year!'

He jokes around, but it would make the show a much less pleasant experience if the cast were not so close – and no two people are closer than Ian and his on-screen brother Paul. 'We love each other,' said Ian. 'We are like brothers. We dress alike, it's kind of freaky but we do have a great rapport. The thing is I realise this: I could be doing this with anyone else. Paul is such a phenomenally talented committed actor, and he's my good friend, and we could be doing this with anybody else and we got lucky. We worked really hard to get these roles and we're going to continue to work even harder to keep them.'

The two were also close in age: Paul was twenty-seven to Ian's thirty-one and were relative veterans of the acting world, having both been around the acting scene since their late teens. They had even appeared on the same shows, such as *Smallville*, though not at the same time. Both left home at an early age to pursue their dream and for both, *The Vampire Diaries* was their biggest success to date. Ian was arguably on a more successful show than *Lost*, but his part in its success was nowhere near as big as in *The Vampire Diaries*. It was only natural then that each could truly appreciate what the other was going through: 'I remember right when we finished shooting those beautiful billboard ads that were everywhere last fall, Paul [Wesley] and I went to a restaurant that's a mutual favourite of ours and we got a bottle of wine and we toasted. I said, "Man, we could have been doing this with anybody else in the world. That would've sucked. But instead, it's us." We've got such a great understanding of each other. Sometimes you come into people's lives for a reason. There's an attraction there, between the energies – we're lucky. I tell these guys just to remember, we are the luckiest kids in Hollywood!'

Of course, the feeling is mutual. Paul told *Dish* magazine: 'At the end of the day, if somebody I cared about called me at four in the morning and said drive two hours because I am stuck, I'll do it. I have like four friends that I'll do it for and Ian is one of them. Ian has the same values as me. We've both been doing this for so long, for 10 years we've been working, so we don't have that naïveté in a sense where we have that seniority. We sort of bond on that level where we can talk from a place like,

"Hey man, isn't this great?" We've been working so hard to get something like this.'

The pair have become so close, it's as if they actually were brothers at heart. They had moved beyond simple friendship and into a territory where they felt comfortable criticising and teasing each other, just as brothers do: 'We didn't know each other at all before we started filming but he's now become one of my closest friends. He's an amazing guy, a fantastic actor and a good person and I really feel that I have a great brotherly thing going with him in real life. All day long we tease each other, mess around, pick on each other and get into heated discussions. It's great.'

The feeling extended to include Nina Dobrev. The three principal cast members spent all day, every day, with each other. Paul told the *LA Times*: 'Nina, Ian and I are together 24 hours a day, seven days a week, other than when we go to bed at night. We just rip on one another in the most affectionate ways, and that's what makes the day go by better. I'm having so much fun.'

'Nina is our little sister in a sense,' he continued to Dish. 'This whole experience is a surprise. It's like having a secret that we didn't tell anyone and we were hoping that they would like it as much as we did. And they did for now! Until people stop watching! The whole experience is amazing. This group of people, our crew, is the most phenomenal crew I've ever met in my career. And this cast, I love and adore them. We have a blast. I have so much respect for them, and have amazing craft service – the best.'

Moving out to Atlanta has been one of the hardest adjustments for some of the cast. Nina Dobrev (Elena) had only just found a place in LA when she found herself on the move once again, this time to Atlanta. And so it was up to some of the natives to make the rest of the cast feel right at home, too. Candice Accola, who plays ditzy Caroline Forbes on the show, was one of those who helped the others adjust. She got along really well with Nina, and Candice opened up her house and family so the rest of the cast could have a few home comforts: 'The whole cast is getting together for barbecues at least once a week. Here in Atlanta, my aunt and uncle have a lake house and we have all gotten together there and gone tubing every weekend, even the producers! It is kind of disgusting how much we get along.'

One thing the barbecues might not be helping is the cast's collective waistlines! 'All first season we complained, "Here we are in the South with all this yummy food," and everyone put on what I like to call a little Southern Comfort, including myself,' laughed Candice, during an interview with *Entertainment Weekly*. It got so bad that the producers had to build the cast an on-site gym – not that they ever got to use it very much! Instead the team prefer to work out outdoors, with the boys kick-boxing, swimming and cycling, while the girls take yoga and go for runs. 'But yeah, no one's stepped foot in that gym. Once you get to work, they get you all dolled up in hair and make-up, and then you sit around for X amount of hours, but you can't just mess up all the hair and make-up department's work, because then it takes all that time to rest. So the gym kinda sits there taunting us.'

With such strict work schedules, there isn't all that much time for bonding but when they do get the chance, the cast goes all out. Often the girls make a special effort to get together for dinner once a week and the boys have gone on a fun road trip to Ohio to see a play-off football game: 'We drove up there, which was, let's say, about a nine-hour drive from Atlanta, just for the game. [We were] in the freezing cold, sat in the bleachers, then drove right back,' Steven R. McQueen (Jeremy Gilbert) told MTV.

And it wasn't just offset that the cast had a lot of fun, but on-set too. Katerina Graham, who plays Bonnie Bennett (a witch whose ancestors came from Salem, Massachusetts) told a teenage fan interviewer about the fun times they had on-set: 'Nina had jumped out of this area and scared the bejezus out of me. That I like, screamed bloody murder and everyone on the set turned around and stared at us and I was like, "Just, just, just playing around, you guys. Get back to work, just joking around!" And I'm like, "Nina, what are you doing?" [laughs] and she laughed and thought it was really funny but then a couple hours later, Ian popped up from behind her while she was talking to me and scared the crap out of her so there's a lot of scaring people on-set. It's kind of ridiculous…'

It's great that the cast are so natural around each other because this really enhances their performance. Candice summed it up to *StarPulse*: '[It] makes the process a little easier. There's that comfort to play around with the scenes. You can go there without feeling like the other person is going to judge you.'

Of course, some of the best fun they had on-set was getting dressed up in period costumes for the flashback scenes where the Salvatore brothers meet Katherine Pierce for the first time, back in the nineteenth century. Jennifer Bryan, the show's costume designer, researched the era in great detail, and got to design period-style outfits for the cast.

'Sometimes I'll have to explain to them: "Well, what is this for?" "People wore this because so and so." I have to give them a little history lesson so they understand what they're wearing, the purpose of it. Back then, a lot of what you wore was determined by your activity. You'd change clothes more often.

You'd have morning clothes, evening clothes. Women of a certain economic stature would change two or three times a day. Not like we do now, throw on jeans and that's it. So this is what you'd wear if you were home, this is what you'd wear if you were coming out of a carriage. [The cast] get into it,' she told *Entertainment Weekly*.

Nina in particular loved getting dressed up. 'Playing Katherine takes so long. Getting into the character, there's the hair and make-up process, and just getting dressed alone takes half an hour because there's corsets and pantaloons. There's so many layers that it takes half an hour to put the outfits on, so I couldn't play both in one day. It's very good because it takes a lot of energy. When I'm in that corset for 17 hours, at the end of the day I feel like I've done a workout. I remember looking at my stomach and thinking, "I should get myself a corset for every day." It really tones you up. You're sucking in, all day,' she told JustJared.buzznet.com. Although she also admitted to *Elle* magazine that after one particularly long day in a corset, she almost passed out from how tight it was!

There have been other times when their on-set experiences haven't been so good, though. 'Make-up's never fun,' Paul told IESB.com. 'Nobody wants to show up at six in the morning to get make-up. The good news is we don't have a lot of make-up [for the show].'

Sometimes it wasn't the make-up, but the weather that caused the problems. 'One memory that wasn't the most pleasant, physically, was when we were shooting and it was below freezing,' Nina told AOL's TV Squad. 'We had to pretend like it was fall, and it was raining the whole episode. At the beginning of one take my hair would be dry and normal, and two minutes later when they called cut, there was ice in my hair because it was so cold. I stayed outside in wet clothes for

12 or 14 hours, and then I got really sick.' Luckily, she was given some time to recover!

Yet for the most part, the cast were having a ball. And it wasn't just the cast who felt like they were part of a new family – this extended to all the producers and the production crew as well. Asked what her favourite moment on-set was, co-creator and executive producer Julie Plec described the night after the pilot 'wrapped' (finished filming). The whole crew rented a party bus, complete with stripper poles. 'But no strippers,' said Paul. They got to dance, celebrate, and really come together as a team. It made them feel buoyant and if ever a cast's enthusiasm and joy could radiate through a television screen and influence an audience, then *The Vampire Diaries* did just that – it wasn't the kind of thing that could be faked: 'People just know what's real and what's not,' Katerina told *LA Times*. 'On our show, we go out of our way to make sure that we connect with everyone. I said before – and this is my Bonnie-ism coming out – the reason that the show is a success [is because of] how we are and the love that we have for each other. And the fans, of course! Without that chemistry and that bond, I don't know how successful the show would be.'

Chapter Eleven

On Location

Elena: Hey, come on! There's more to me than just gloomy graveyard girl. There's a whole another Elena you have yet to meet. (1.3, 'Friday Night Bites')

Georgia is a highly atmospheric place with a rich local history. The real-life locations used by the show lend a certain gothic authenticity to the experience that a purpose-built set in the back lot of a Hollywood studio just wouldn't have been able to replicate. Jessica Royal from Bonanza Productions (who produced the show alongside Warner Brothers) said: 'When the writers came and visited Covington and saw the square, it was exactly what they had pictured for Mystic Falls.' As a state, Georgia was trying to establish itself as a film-friendly place and offered tax credit incentives to entice film-makers.

Yet there was more than just savings to be made by moving down to the Deep South. The crew had access to some beautiful, ready-made sets, such as Glenridge Hall in

Sandy Springs, Georgia, which was built in 1929 and has its own mile-long driveway and 47 acres of forest. Glenridge's faux-Tudor front stands in for the exterior of the Salvatore house, while Gaither Plantation is used for the interior. On location, there were even rumours of hauntings: 'Recently we were filming on a real plantation – it was creepy as there was a lot of dark history. After slavery was abolished, the owner of that plantation was the first guy to be hung because he lynched all his slaves instead of setting them free. So he was hanged and now the place is historically, famously listed as one of the most haunted places in the US. We filmed there at night time and it was just really weird and creepy. All of the graves were there, about 150 of them – it was very bizarre. I'm very practical and don't believe in the paranormal, but I do believe your imagination is a powerful thing and everyone on-set got very jumpy,' Paul Wesley told Gaydar Nation.

Because of the show's heavy production schedule, most of the cast did not get to see much of the city beyond where they were shooting. The show is actually set in a small town just outside of Atlanta, called Covington, Georgia. There, the set pieces actually remain part of the town, even when the show is not airing. Some enterprising locals decided to set up *The Vampire Diaries*-themed tours of 'Mystic Falls' (aka Covington), called 'Vampire Stalkers', where fans can visit some of the key shooting locations such as the Mystic Grill, the Lockwood Mansion, the cemetery and the Gilbert household. If you're ever in the Covington, Georgia area, make sure you check it out!

Kevin Williamson has been a little disappointed by how little he's been able to see of nearby Atlanta, though: 'We've been to a lot of places around Atlanta, but still haven't discovered as much of the city as we'd like to because we film 15-hour days. But when we do go out, I love that there are so many diverse pockets to explore, from Buckhead and Inman Park to Little 5 Points, which has that awesome urban edge.'

Unfortunately, some of the cast members got on the wrong side of the Atlanta Police Department while shooting promotional photographs on a bridge over a highway. On 11 September, 2009 Nina Dobrev, Kayla Ewell, Sara Canning, Krystal Vayda (a fellow actress who does not appear in *The Vampire Diaries*), Candice Accola and her boyfriend, photographer Tyler Shields, were all booked for disorderly conduct after motorists complained about distracting flashes from the camera. The charges were subsequently dropped and the cast released after each posted a bond. It was a misunderstanding quickly resolved.

However, that didn't mean the media didn't have a field day with the story. After all, this was the amazing *The Vampire Diaries'* cast, whose young actors and actresses seemed like paradigms of virtue – great role models for teens. The media was itching to poke holes in the seemingly perfect exterior and once they found the smallest opportunity, they leapt on it, claiming that it was a very different kind of flashing from the girls that had caused the complaint. For many of the cast members, this was an eye-opener and especially for Nina Dobrev, who was outraged by the story the media had concocted: 'When I read something like that and see how much is fabricated, it makes me second-guess what I read in those magazines,' she told *Nylon* magazine. 'It's weird, because I'm me, and my friends see me as the girl who they hang out with and go to the movies with. And all of a sudden I'm in all those magazines. Even I would get my nails done and read the gossip magazines. I remember growing up and watching movies, and thinking that these weren't real people – they're just dolls. But [stories like the one concerning the arrest] make me realize how much sensationalism exists in the media. Now, I take it with a grain of salt. I want to be respected and known for the work I do, and not for the life that I lead.' It didn't dent Nina's love of the city though, although she would take extra care in the future to keep out of the city's police department!

It was Paul Wesley, in particular, who had a strange relationship with Atlanta. Being there meant he was apart from a lot of the things he loved – like his family, who were up in New Jersey, and his fiancée, actress Torrey DeVitto – and he was unable to partake in some of his favourite sports, like skiing and ice hockey. But, like Ian, Paul has an adventurous spirit and relished the new opportunity to try something outside of his comfort zone: 'I feel weird being inland,' he told Zimbio, 'that's odd for me – I miss the water, that's the only thing. The thing I love about being an actor is the ability to travel and experience new cultures. I filmed a bit in Charleston, but I don't know much about the South. I can now say that I've lived on the East Coast, I've lived on the West Coast, I've lived in the South, I've lived in Canada. It's nice to have the freedom to experience that while I'm young.'

Ian, on the other hand, was very happy to be back Down South. 'That night air in Georgia is just like Louisiana, it smells like when I was a kid. That sense-memory is so powerful,' he told Nola.com. He wasn't far from his family in Louisiana and felt comfortably back home. And his mom even helped him move: 'She flew from New Orleans to Los Angeles, to Santa Monica, to help me get out of my house and get it ready to rent it out. She helped me pack up, and got in the car and drove with me across country with my kitties.'

'I can fly home to be with my family all the time. I can go fishing in the Florida Keys. I can just disappear and it's quick,' he continued on the benefits of being in Georgia to *Coup De Main* magazine.

One thing he didn't like so much, however, were the stunts they had to perform on-set: 'One time I had to jump backwards off a building and drop on to a thick pad. The fall was only about six feet but it felt so scary. It took me forever to do it – I felt like such a baby.'

Maybe he did have reason to be somewhat apprehensive, though: accidents and mishaps were pretty common on *The Vampire Diaries'* set. 'Oh yeah, we're plagued,' Julie Plec told *Entertainment Weekly*, 'plagued with injury. Nina [Dobrev] threw her back out and was sidelined for weeks. And then Paul Wesley fell and twisted his ankle and has been in a boot.'

The accident Paul suffered was, quite literally, completely out of character for him. It happened early December 2010: 'I was running down the street in a pair of boots in LA, and it was raining and I had an umbrella, and whatever, I fell on the kerb. It's ridiculous. I wish I had a better story for you – I wish I could have told you that I karate-kicked an assailant but unfortunately, it was my own stupidity and clumsiness. Very anti-Stefan. I think that would be great if Stefan was running down the street and he sprained his ankle; that would humanise him a little bit, you know.' In the event, the accident delayed shooting and Paul spent over three weeks on crutches.

But then a similar accident befell Kevin Williamson. 'I Facebook'd my emergency room pictures,' he laughed. 'I was at the hotel in Atlanta and I didn't want to wake anybody up, and so I finally crawled down to the lobby and said, "Get me a cab. I need to go to the emergency room!" I had completely messed my ankle up. Overnight it had swelled up. I couldn't walk. It was the most painful thing in the world... all because I stumbled on the steps. I did the same sort of manoeuvre as Paul, twisted it the wrong way.'

Of course, it wasn't such a problem for Kevin – at least he could sit and write all day, keeping the pressure off his ankle to heal properly. Paul wasn't offered that same luxury: as the old adage goes, the show must go on. While Kevin was sympathetic to the plight of his actor, he couldn't do anything to relieve Paul's pain and so they carried on filming: 'The problem with Paul's [ankle] was his never got to heal because he kept having to stand on it and walk on it, and act on it so he never truly got to stay off of it. That's why it took forever to get him off the crutches. We would go in and stand him up there and then take the crutches away, and he'd do the scene and then "Cut!" and someone would run in with the crutches.' So much for sympathy!

Meanwhile, Ian was hardly immune to injury either. He was diagnosed with pneumonia in late 2010, which lasted for two months. 'I had to do ADR [Advance Dialogue Recording] on four episodes extensively. Two episodes I had to loop completely. Literally, almost every single word I said. It was a battle. There was nothing I could do. When you can't breathe out of your nose, or you have a mouth full of cough drops so you're not coughing through the entire scene, it makes it difficult. I'm not making excuses for any kind of bad performance, but it just levelled me, and it levelled Damon but it's gone, and I'm done with it.' It particularly affected episode 12 in Season Two, called 'The Descent': 'It was a very emotional Damon episode, and I just wouldn't allow [myself to be sick]. I literally sat in my sauna for over an hour a day and sweated everything out,' he told *Entertainment Weekly*.

Of course certain injuries were inevitable with a vampire show, too – like bite marks! 'I've had marks left on me from when Ian actually did bite me,' Kayla Ewell told *TV Guide* magazine. 'We definitely have battle scars.'

'When one of the actors bites someone, they have to put fake blood in their mouth, and it's gross and sticky and disgusting,' she continued. 'Pretty much all of us have tasted the blood at some point. It's a good thing we have nice showers in our trailers, because we're constantly showering after every scene.' They also had fangs to deal with. For Ian and Paul, this was a particularly painful process as they had to deal with the earliest incarnations of the fangs, along with contact lenses and hours in the make-up chair. Ian described the effect: 'The contacts are what really sell it. You have these huge, full-eye contacts with the colour of the eye visible – those are a bit difficult to get in. You cry for about five minutes. Get a nice little airbrush of red around the eyes and you pop in the fangs and there's a shift – I become a completely different person.' They could only put the fangs in right before they went in for the bite though, as they would have sounded pretty silly talking with extra teeth in their mouths. Despite this, Ian used to insist that he could say the Gettysburg Address with his fangs in!

As the show grew more successful, the budget became a little bigger and the special effects team had a bit more time: they were able to ease up on the physical aspects of being a vampire and develop more of the effects in post-production. 'We started out with these crazy fangs that were moulded and then we all talked and so finally they're CGI fangs, which are much easier,' Paul told Rachel Ray on *The Rachel Ray Show*. Even with CGI fangs, Kevin Williamson and his team were determined not to go too overboard with the visual effects, especially as they wouldn't have the luxury of months of post-production, unlike a movie.

'We want to do something a little more subtle and just keep it to some sort of biological, sort of physiological response, so when they get excited we just sort of see the blood rush under the skin,' Kevin revealed to *CanMag*. 'Pale their face out a little bit, but it all goes to the eye and they kind of have these bloody eyes. Then, of course, they have teeth. But we wanted to do something just to keep it sort of simple, something we can manage and actually do a good job with every week.' This did mean, however, that the cast had to walk around with little dots around their eyes to help the CGI. 'They put these four dots on my face for the CGI guys to use as markers in post-production – I think that's how they do it in *True Blood* as well. It's actually very funny because we do these scenes and Nina has to pretend to be in love with me, and I'm standing there with polka-dots on my face,' Paul Wesley told the *LA Times*.

Another thing they improved was the taste (and nutritional value) of the fake blood. In the beginning, this was pure, red-dyed corn syrup. Connor McCullagh described to *Seventeen* magazine how they made the blood initially: 'The blood we used I make myself. I use edible corn syrup, food colouring, some salt as a preservative, and some peppermint extract to make it a little more palatable. I usually make a few gallons at a time, and on a show like this it lasts, you know, two or three months.' In one episode, Paul had to pretend to drink an entire glass of it. He was so committed to the role that he actually did down the whole thing without pouring any of it away, which is what most actors would have done. Gross! Thankfully, the blood is tastier now!

All told, it was such a fun atmosphere with such a great cast and crew that no one had anything bad to say about the experience. 'Paul, Ian and Nina are in that first-season euphoria right now that is so contagious,' laughed Kevin, 'but it's really a blast. I'm having a lot of fun. I haven't been this excited about something in a really long time – it feels like we have something really special here.'

Chapter Twelve

The Big Wide World

Damon: You're dead, dude. Get over it. (1.04, 'Family Ties')

It's almost impossible to believe but *The Vampire Diaries* didn't come to the UK until well into the first season in the US when it was picked up by the network ITV2, home of *Gossip Girl*, *American Idol* and *The Only Way is Essex*. The first episode aired in February 2010. Yet with *Twilight* fever gripping the nation, *True Blood* impressing the critics and the BBC's own *Being Human* (a show about three room-mates who happen to be a vampire, a werewolf and a ghost, all trying to live normal human lives) fulfilling the 'quirky' angle, was there any room for another vampire show?

Anything that garners so much buzz in the US was going to spark an interest with UK television viewers, though. The downside to the pre-show buzz was that a large proportion of the UK audience (aka internet-savvy teens) were already well informed and eager to watch the show. The result was that ITV2 had to contend with huge amounts of digital piracy. According to *Nylon* magazine, *The Vampire Diaries* was the most illegally downloaded show in the UK at the time of its official airing.

To ITV2's credit, they attempted to curb this digital piracy tsunami by trying something that had never been done before: they put the first 10 episodes of *The Vampire Diaries* online on their iTunes store for £1.89 for the standard version and £2.49 (HD version) before airing them on TV so that keen fans could legally get a head-start. They would then offer the last 12 episodes the day after they aired on the US. 'We're committed to providing our shows with the best possible launch platform,' said Josh Berger, president of Warner Bros Entertainment UK. 'The highly innovative approach to releasing *The Vampire Diaries* gives us and ITV2 the chance to maximise excitement ahead of its UK premiere in February, and provides consumers with a high-quality legal alternative to pirated versions.'

ITV2 had already had some success with US properties such as *Gossip Girl* and *Entourage*, but they had only ever put download-to-own content on their iTunes store after the show already aired so this was a chance to build the buzz even more among the core fans: 'By making *The Vampire Diaries* available in the ITV2 area on iTunes we're feeding the appetite for brand new US content and helping to spread the word about a show we're incredibly excited about,' said Zai Bennett, ITV director of digital channels and acquisitions. As more teens become comfortable with downloading and watching shows on their computers, this was a key strategic move for ITV.

ITV2 and Warner Bros (parent company of The CW) threw everything behind this promotion, even bringing the cast over for a huge event at the Apple Store on London's Regent Street on 12 December 2009. Although the show hadn't yet aired, thousands of fans packed out the store to ask Ian, Paul and Nina their burning questions. The event really proved to Ian that he had made it: 'It's fun and flattering,' he told *Metro*. 'We shot some pictures at the Mac store the other day and they gave me an amazing computer. When Mac gives you stuff, you know you've made it – they don't have to give things away.' They also did the British media rounds, appearing on BBC Radio 1, *This Morning*, in nationwide newspapers and magazines, on the red carpet at the *Sherlock Holmes* movie premiere and at Elton John's charity ball (rumoured to be costing the network £2,000-a-head for an invite). Nina was astounded by the reception they received – and even a little star-struck by a fellow Canadian actress who was in town at the same time: 'Rachel McAdams is staying at the same hotel we are; how cool is that?' she told *Nylon*.

ITV2 went all out with competitions too, offering up a trip to London to watch an advance screening of the season finale by asking fans to dress themselves up as vampires for a chance to win.

When *The Vampire Diaries* finally aired in the UK on 2 February 2010, the ratings were excellent, with over 980,000 viewers on its first night. For a comparable US debut, *Caprica*, which aired on Sky1 on the same night, had only 169,000 people tune in.

Reviews for *The Vampire Diaries* followed a similar pattern to the US. The pilot received mixed critical acclaim, with some reviewers claiming they had 'fang fatigue' (*This is Leicestershire*), while others were a little deterred by the show's tone: 'It's spectacularly earnest and 90s-looking, but since it's been created by Kevin Williamson, of *Scream* and *Dawson's Creek* fame, that's not a huge surprise.' (*Guardian*). Yet the *Guardian* review also acknowledged that advanced information from the US proved the show would only get better as the season went on, '*The Vampire Diaries* is a mishmash of ideas we've seen before (a ring allowing a vampire to withstand daylight? Hello, Buffy), brooding bad boys and clunking bad-emo-band dialogue about souls. Though its teen target audience might not necessarily cross over with *True Blood*, it still suffers by comparison. In the same way that *Scream* upended trite horror films by poking fun at their conventions, *True Blood* makes crows and pointed silences and eyeliner seem dated. But this dip in quality doesn't mean there's no, ahem, life in the old vampire yet – and given how well *The Vampire Diaries* has done in the US, there's probably still life in the series too.'

The *Independent* was even more magnanimous in its praise: 'With the genre approaching critical mass, can *The Vampire Diaries* really offer anything worth turning on for? The answer, perhaps surprisingly, is yes. It might not be the most groundbreaking show on television right now, but it's a well-crafted, interestingly developed series, which really kicks up a gear after an anodyne opening episode.' Metro praised it, too: 'It's far more teen-friendly than its steamy cousin *True Blood* but with sexy leads and credible small-town anxieties, *The Vampire Diaries* is a gripping addition to the genre.'

All told, it was a great reception in a market verging on oversaturation – and proof that *The Vampire Diaries* was doing more than just riding on the coat-tails of *Twilight* and *True Blood*... it had the individuality and flair to create its own place in the market.

Of course, the UK wasn't the only place where *The Vampire Diaries* hit it big. The cast got to travel Down Under to Australia on an International Press Tour, where Nina and Ian were able to take some time off together on a trip to Queensland's Port

Douglas for a Reef and Rainforest adventure. That certainly sparked some rumours that the two were dating, although they both vehemently denied it! Nina was visiting a friend out there too, a girl named Ash: 'Ian, Ash and I took a full day, dived three times and saw things we'd only seen on the Discovery Channel. The Coral, sharks, Nemo! We found him – he told us to tell the world that he's all good now. Haha! The whole thing was breathtaking.'

And their popularity wasn't confined to English-speaking countries either: they have a huge fanbase in Spain, and Ian and Paul headed there for a conference called BloodNightCon, *The Vampire Diaries'* Convention in Barcelona. They have a following in the Philippines too, with the *Philippine Daily Inquirer* reviewing the show: 'What's not to like? You've got a ridiculously good-looking cast, vampires, witches, and a love triangle that is deliciously screwing with your mind.'

I think that sums it up pretty well!

Chapter Thirteen

Coming Up On: *The Vampire Diaries*

Damon: He has no idea what normal is, his entire existence isn't normal. Normal to a vampire is drinking human blood. But he spent all this time fighting it, when he should've been learning how to control it and now it's controlling him instead. (1.19, 'Miss Mystic Falls')

In the summer of 2010, The CW officially confirmed that there was to be a second season of *The Vampire Diaries*. It was the news that the fans, as well as the cast and crew, had all been anxiously waiting for, even though with the incredible ratings and reviews this was basically a given.

Paul Wesley had a theory about why the first season had been such a huge hit: 'The evolution of the show is what's made it so successful. Actually, even with the pilot episode I thought we were establishing interesting characters – but if we hadn't kept evolving, I think it might have become really old, really fast. There's a good balance of humour, evil, darkness and light, and the characters are not one-dimensional. The show also has amazing cinematography and an awesome score. It becomes addictive, even for people who aren't into the genre,' he told *WetPaint.com*.

Now that they knew the show was a success, The CW could really throw some money behind the advertising. During the first season, the advertising and poster campaigns had focused on the love-triangle aspect of the show and were quite romantic in feel. The major tag line was also quite tame: 'Love Sucks', the posters read. The three leads peered broodingly out of the glossy print ads, Elena (Nina Dobrev) caught between the two brothers – for the most part, not touching either of them. But for the second season, the marketers at The CW really decided to switch things up a bit. Perhaps to draw in more *True Blood* fans than *Twilight*, they amped up the sex appeal. Billboards appeared with Elena in a sexy black dress draped over the two brothers, while lying on a bed, skin glistening, big hair messily tousled. Yet it was the tag line that caused the most controversy. 'CATCH VD,' the ads screamed. It made several motorists do a double-take, that's for sure!

That tag line also upset some of their more sensitive viewers as well as some parents, who believed that *The Vampire Diaries* was meant to be more family-friendly than its HBO counterpart. 'VD simply stands for "Vampire Diaries" and anyone who thinks otherwise should probably get themselves checked out,' said a representative for The CW in an innuendo-laden statement in response to the complaints. But it certainly got people talking, which was what the publicity intended. It wasn't the first time that The CW had courted controversy either. In print ads for their show *Gossip Girl*, they had used the tag line 'OMFG', which had also angered the Parents Television Council.

They weren't planning to stop, though. In fact, the next ads were even racier. In video teasers for the show, some of the sexiest clips were thrown together along with the shout-line: 'Got Wood?' (referring to the wooden stakes to kill vampires, what were you thinking?!).

If *The Vampire Diaries'* team was looking for attention, then they certainly got it.

Season Two of the show was Kevin Williamson and Julie Plec's chance to really start to delve deep into the mythology of the town and the way people related to each other that are so crucial to the heart of the show. Damon and Elena's relationship is an interesting one and certainly something that appealed to Kevin and Julie on reading the books: 'One of the things that I really like about L.J. Smith's books is that it took a very long time for Elena and Damon to reach any kind of detente, any kind of true connection with each other. I want to make sure that we take our own sweet time with that as well, because you have to believe it,' Julie told *Soap Opera Weekly*. 'Every now and then, Elena will get the tiniest little glimpse of what we'll call "the softer side of Damon", but there's not going to be any true love blooming anytime soon. That's the fun of it. It's waiting and waiting, and dissecting every little time he does something nice for her and how it makes her feel – that anticipation, that build-up.' The love triangle isn't the only thing that's going to develop – in fact, it's about to build up into a love square once Katherine gets more involved!

It was also a chance to develop some of the lesser characters and really get behind the scenes of what was going on with Tyler Lockwood (and the werewolf connection), Bonnie Bennett (with her growing witchy powers), Caroline Forbes (can she remain innocent for too much longer?) and the rest. 'Our goal for Season Two is to integrate our smaller characters into our triangle, there's always ways that we can integrate our characters better,' said Julie on the VRO radio show. The other big question that will continue to be asked is why Elena and Katherine look identical – not just similar (as they are in the books) but true doppelgängers. It was already established in Season One that they were both of the Pierce bloodline, but the mystery is about to deepen. Exciting stuff!

For Kevin Williamson and Julie Plec, the future is bright. Kevin isn't about to make the same mistake again and turn away from his core fans and the voice he clearly writes best for – the teens. He's in the midst of producing a few additional shows for The CW, along with his movies *Scream 4* and possibly, *Scream 5*. The CW optioned another one of L.J. Smith's series, *The Secret Circle* (read more about the books on the Stefan side), and again, Kevin was brought on board. Young actress Brittany Robertson has been cast as the lead role, Cassie, and as of publication, the pilot was scheduled to begin shooting by the end of 2011.

Yet whatever Kevin decides to do, it's clear he won't be leaving *The Vampire Diaries* any time soon. That's not to say that we can't fear for the rest of the cast, though! 'Sometimes the death of a favourite character is necessary to achieve the best emotional and dramatic punch,' said Julie, who has already proved that the writing team won't pull any punches, 'Kevin and I like to say all the time no one is safe on the show.'

Chapter Fourteen

Environmental Superhero

Damon: I came into this town wanting to destroy it. Tonight I found myself wanting to protect it. (1.22, 'Founder's Day')

If Ian Somerhalder could pinpoint a real life-changing moment, it wouldn't be getting cast as Damon: it would be Hurricane Katrina. It awoke in him a deep-rooted desire to make a difference, not just through his words or his wallet but through his deeds and dedication.

Ian has always loved the environment. He can trace his love of the great outdoors right back to the values his mother instilled in him about staying healthy and living in harmony with the world around him. But in recent years, he has taken this a step further. He is well aware of the power of celebrity and conscious about putting his influence to good use. In the aftermath of Hurricane Katrina, he had stepped timidly into the waters of environmental and political activism but it still couldn't prepare him for what was to come.

Ian's home state of Louisiana is one of the most delicate and vulnerable ecological systems in the USA. There are thousands of square miles of swampland, marshes and barrier islands lying along the Gulf of Mexico and the Mississippi River. When he was growing up, they were Ian's playground and he has many fond memories of romping around the marshes with his BB gun, or riding through the fields on the back of his favourite horse. His beloved marshlands came under threat just as the shooting for Season One of *The Vampire Diaries* wrapped. Ian was headed back to Mandeville, Louisiana for a welcome break and some home comforts – like his mum's delicious, home-cooked, healthy meals. He was prepared for rest and relaxation, and not a lot else.

Then, on 20 April 2010, word of a crisis in the Gulf of Mexico broke in the mainstream media. An explosion at the BP rig Deepwater Horizon killed 11 men and permanently damaged the drilling platform. As a result, the equivalent of millions of barrels of oil flowed unchecked into the water. The Deepwater Horizon oil spill (also known as the BP oil spill and the Gulf Oil crisis) would go on to become one of the biggest ecological disasters ever to hit the United States and was by far the greatest accidental marine oil spill to have occurred in the history of the petroleum industry. For three months, oil flowed into the Gulf of Mexico, causing extensive harm to wildlife habitats and incalculable damage to the valuable fishing and tourism industries in and around the Gulf, including Ian's home state.

Ian was outraged and although due to return to Los Angeles, he was equally determined not to go anywhere. 'I'm just scared right now,' he told *USA Today*. 'No one really knows what's happening. From what we see on the surface, NOAA and the oceanographers can estimate what's coming out of the rig but BP has denied scientists access to the footage of the gushing leak below the surface, so there's no way for us to know the actual realistic scale of the damage that's still happening. NOAA is a government administration! Why isn't [President Barack] Obama stepping in and demanding that footage, demanding a live view of what's going on?' It was one of the first times he'd ever really allowed a political agenda to enter his environmental activism.

This wasn't just talk, either: he filmed a PSA [Public Service Announcement] for the Audubon Institute, a New Orleans-based zoological society that helped to clean up animals and birds found affected by the oil and was trying to protect some of the more fragile species, such as the sea turtles: 'What's going to happen is, there's going to be a massive wildlife clean-up recovery effort, and that's where most of the help and donations will be needed.'

Of course, it was to have an impact on more than animals and birds. 'It's not just because it's my home [that's affected],' he continued to *USA Today*. 'Just watching all these very proud, hardworking fishermen, who have never asked for anything in their lives, who support themselves and their families for generations with this one industry now it's likely to disappear. If it'll ever recover, we're talking decades and decades. It's beyond tragic.'

He was upset by the lack of interest from the normally activism-heavy Hollywood set. His anger was so great that he feared saying something he would come to regret and so he banned himself from Twitter for a while in case he might unleash his anger in a destructive and less-than-professional manner. 'Coming from the entertainment world, I'm really shaken by how quiet Hollywood is and I say that out of respect for my peers and colleagues, but I'm really bummed that no one is really coming up to help the situation. I think a telethon is a good way to funnel money into these channels. We need to set one of those things up to really paint a picture of exactly how much devastation is here.' Not one to rest on his laurels, especially for a cause as important as this, he organised a two-hour telethon called 'Disaster in the Gulf: How You Can Help' shown on *Larry King Live* and raised over $2 million.

Even with the money raised, he knew most of the damage was irrevocable and this made him impossibly sad. 'To me and to the people that go down there, [it's] one of the most beautiful places in the world and I actually had to watch it destroyed. And it will be destroyed – forever. My great-grandchildren will not be able to enjoy the Gulf Coast of Louisiana the way I have.'

Activism surrounding the Gulf Oil crisis has brought about some of his most high profile appearances, but it's definitely not the only time he's thrown himself behind a charitable cause. Ian also supports the largest humane society in Louisiana, the St. Tammany Humane Society. He used innovative techniques to help draw his fans to the organisation, such as offering a personalised headshot if you donated $50 and arranging a benefit dinner called 'Bash on the Bayou'. The best part was that he, and the charities he was helping, actually began to see results: 'I can't tell you how thankful I am. When I pull up to the humane society and the car makes noise on the gravel, all the animals freak out and you realise just how many animals are there because of the decibel level. Then you walk by and they're so adorable; they just want love. They don't want to attack you, they want to lick you. They just want interaction. To think that because of this money and because of the efforts of so many *Vampire Diaries'* fans, those animals will be able to find homes and treatments – it's amazing.'

There are lots of celebrities who put their name to causes or donate some of their income, but Ian is even more dedicated than most. But it just wasn't enough for him to donate his cash or even some of his time to the charities he supported and so in late 2010, he decided to set up his own foundation: the IS Foundation. The mission statement on their website reads as follows: 'The IS Foundation aims to empower, educate and collaborate with people and projects to positively impact the planet and its creatures', and on 10 April, 2011, after months of hard work on Ian's part, the IS Foundation was awarded non-profit status. It's a brand new venture for Ian, but one that will enable him to tie all of his passions together: the environment, animal protection and empowering youth. What's more, he's been blown away by the support so far: 'The amount of support for this foundation goes above and beyond,' he told *JustJared.com*. 'Obviously it's invariably difficult to raise money in a time of economic depression which we're about to get into, but it's so inspiring. Put it this way: a six-year-old girl sent me an e-mail saying she gave our foundation her tooth fairy money to help save the planet and it blew my mind. She asked what she can do to help and I just thought that this girl is going to be the President one day.'

Having his own charitable foundation has changed Ian's life forever. For him, acting has now become a means to an end, a way for him to truly attempt to save the planet. Work for the Foundation will take him around the world, too: 'I'm not going to get to do Africa this year, but I am going to be in Central and South America. We'll be going with the Global Alliance for Conservation, which is one of the largest environmental protection organisations in the world. Don Cheadle and I have signed on to be the two spokesperson [sic] for this. I'm going to Central and South America to look at the areas hit hard by deforestation and to figure out how to reforest them sustainably, efficiently and economically to find ways to put people to work. I actually can't sleep at night sometimes and I would go on my own Foundation's website and find more factors.'

If you want to support Ian's foundation, go to www.isfoundation.com to find out how you can help.

Although the protection of animals and the environment are two of the most important issues to Ian, he also worries about the state of health and nutrition, especially in the US. He can't make the whole world drink 10 cups of green tea a day, but he can try to bring attention to some of the more artificial ways we process our food: 'You know, bad cooking scares me. Instead of saying bad food, microwaves. Because it's ruining our cultures, it's ruining our bodies – it changes the integrity of the protein, it changes the molecular structure [of the food] and our bodies digest it differently, and it's just killing us.'

For Ian, his body is his temple: 'Health is wealth. When you're not taking care of yourself, your work reflects it, everything about you reflects it, and I unfortunately don't have the time any more. I have to take care of myself, I'm a major outdoor dude. Whenever I can, I'm out hiking, biking, skiing – I mean, I'm out there, it's just right now, and I'm not complaining in any way, shape or form, we do nothing but work.'

As if to prove he wasn't going to let his work slip away from his values, Ian found a way to get *The Vampire Diaries* involved in his green revolution: 'I just became involved with a very strong green energy company that produces portable, mobile green power. The company's called Go Green Mobile Power. Our first prototype is going to be done in a few days. Go Green Mobile Power will create portable solar/wind/biodiesel generators for use in the film and event industry (as well as other arenas) to replace the off-grid dirty energy that's traditionally used on location,' he told *Zap2it.com*. 'It takes a lot of power to run a movie set. We go through a lot of fuel. It's harmful, and we can start changing that a little bit. We can get rid of these noisy, stinky, disgusting gas generators. There's going to be a lot of thought that goes into this revolution that's going to happen.'

His passion is contagious and certainly seems to have spread to the rest of *The Vampire Diaries'* cast. Ian has helped many of them get involved in similar passions, including one that is close to the heart of the entire cast: The Trevor Project. It's a 24-hour, free confidential suicide hotline for gay and questioning teens who have been bullied, abused or are generally depressed and just need to hear a friendly voice. Ian, Katerina Graham (Bonnie on the show) and Candice Accola (Caroline) filmed a PSA together in support of the project, with the message 'It Will Get Better'. It was all about showing youths that although it might seem unlikely at times, things will improve and there is no need to think of suicide as an option. Other cast members such as Paul Wesley (Stefan) support the Project in an entirely different way – for example, by attending events in the charity's benefit.

Kevin Williamson, who is gay himself, would love to bring more diversity to *The Vampire Diaries'* set. 'It's one of those things that needs to feel organic and seamless,' he observed on the Television Critics Association press tour. 'I don't want it to be a character that comes in and is a one-off. I want someone to come in and have a reason and a purpose and really push that story forward the way I want to do it, and they're so important to the story that without them, the show won't happen. That's what I want.' The more shows such as *The Vampire Diaries* bring awareness of the issues facing teens to the fore, the more likely it is that they will get involved and really begin to make a difference when it comes to society's attitudes towards issues like homophobia, animal cruelty and the destruction of the environment.

One thing is for certain: Ian is a real celebrity who cares and it's clear that wherever his future leads him, his passion for the world we live in isn't going to go anywhere.

Chapter Fifteen

A Future on the Bayou

Damon: My father never approved of anyone I dated. Which made me want them even more, of course.
(1.13, 'Children of the Damned')

Between his environmental activism, charity work and highly demanding role in *The Vampire Diaries* – if he's not shooting five days a week, then he's on the road doing publicity – it's a wonder Ian has time for other projects at all, let alone a love life. He's rumoured to be single at the moment, but it sounds as if any girl would be lucky to have him. He told *Cosmopolitan* what he would do to woo a date: 'I [would] cook for her. They say the way to a man's heart is through his stomach. It's the same way with women or at least the ones I want to be with. And I once flew to Paris to see someone for a matter of hours – just to have lunch.' He even described to *Black Book* magazine what his ultimate seduction playlist tracks would be: 'Next Girl' by The Black Keys, 'Desire Lines' by Deerhunter, 'Lover I Don't Have to

Love' by Bright Eyes, '6669 (I Don't Know If You Know)' by Neon Indian, 'The Gaudy Side of Town' by Gayngs, 'History' by The Verve, 'I Want the World to Stop' by Belle & Sebastian and finally, 'The Recluse' by Cursive. His turn-off is clear: 'Someone who hates animals. I work with the Humane Society a lot and have three rescue cats. I don't care how hot a girl is – if she doesn't like animals, it would be a major, major problem.'

No time for love, maybe, yet he was somehow able to fit in two movies while juggling *The Vampire Diaries* and *Lost* at the same time. The first was a straight-to-DVD feature called *How to Make Love to a Woman*, which fell into the college-comedy genre, about a guy who attempts to save his relationship with his girlfriend by honing his bedroom skills. It starred Josh Meyers (from *That '70s Show*), Krysten Ritter (*Confessions of a Shopaholic*) and former porn star Jenna Jameson. 'I wasn't in much of the film, but it was a really fun little experience,' said Ian. 'The guy [Scott Culver] who directed that is, I think, going to be a great director, and it was a lot of fun working with Krysten Ritter, who I adore and is a wildly talented individual.' However, the film didn't receive great reviews and was described as 'a parade of the familiar from the first frame to the last, rendering the glory of love as a laborious and smug nightmare' by DVD Talk, with DVD Verdict even going so far as to say: 'although there's nothing that sticks out to make it a bad film, not even good performances and a few laughs can overcome the generic mess of the plot. Worth a rental for the truly desperate rom-com fan, but otherwise not for most viewers.'

His next project, which is currently scheduled for early 2012, is a gothic-romance-meets psychological-thriller – *Cradlewood* – directed by Harry Weinmann, a visual effects designer-turned-director. In this, Ian plays the handsome heir to a substantial fortune. He has everything a man could want in life: lots of money, charisma and a beautiful woman but everything changes when his partner falls pregnant. He subsequently discovers that his family has been cursed after one of his ancestors made a pact with a demon and when his son is born, he will die.

The producers of the movie are aiming high. One producer, Michel Shane, said: 'We see this as almost like an American-style *Pan's Labyrinth* in look and feel. It's a perfect segue for the kids who have outgrown *Twilight* but want something romantic and scary. Our monster will be quite terrifying; she is sexually attractive and monstrous at the same time.' Based on the enticing synopsis and that quote, who knows what the monstrous twist will be? Whatever it may be, it seems as if Ian won't be straying too far from his supernatural-romance loving fan base. For him, the movie also meant another opportunity for adventure as it was filmed in Melbourne, Australia over the summer of 2010.

They're not exactly the deep-and-meaningful roles that Ian envisioned for himself, but he has become much more philosophical as of late: 'I started reading in-depth philosophy way too young, Nietzsche, Freud, listening to Wagner – I dove a little too deep for too many years, but the lighter books on that were heavy-handed as far as psychology. One book that I really loved [is a] book Colin Wilson wrote called *The Outside*. I remember reading all this philosophy and all these great stories, tall-tale stories, everything from Shakespeare on up, and I think Colin Wilson helped me understand. For every 25-year-old guy, you should just read this book, because it really helped me understand a lot of the books I had been reading for so many years, and that changed my life in a big way.'

For Ian, his unexpected (and unintended) career break post-*Lost* brought his career into perspective and he found himself turning to the giants of philosophy to get him through. He's even had part of that philosophy tattooed on his skin: Hic et Nunc, which translates from Latin as 'Here and Now', which is printed indelibly on the inside of his right forearm. It's a small reminder to always to live in the present and to enjoy the life that he has. While he may have wanted to only work on Big Important Movies or small, critically acclaimed independents, for him this doesn't seem to be where the work is. He's come to terms with the fact that, given his model good looks and teen-heart-throb laden CV, he might find himself confined to similar roles.

Yet this is something he cannot change so he instead throws time and effort into things he can change, projects like his activism and his charities. He sees his career for what it is: his day job. But his passions are what spill out into the rest of his life.

That's not to say that he doesn't love *The Vampire Diaries*. 'I say this not complaining – I'm elated – but there's nothing else I could possibly do than what I'm doing right now,' he admits. Indeed, the show has opened up so many doors for him and enabled him to play bad boy Damon, the absolute best character on television at the moment. And it doesn't look as if *The Vampire Diaries* is about to slow down any time soon, which means Ian will be gracing our screens for a long time to come.

Yet ultimately, Ian's dream is perhaps different to that of his fans. He spoke honestly to NOLA.com about what he saw for his future: 'My dream, to be honest with you, at some point soon I want to own a really great house in New Orleans that I can go to with my family, tons of property on the bayou where I grew up – on the Tchefuncte or on the lake; those are my roots. I would like to spend about six years on [*The Vampire Diaries*] and do a couple of movies, and then cash out and spend the rest of my life on a horse.'

Chapter Sixteen

Vampire Tweets

Elena: I'm not going to be one of those pathetic girls whose world stops spinning because of some guy. (1.05, 'You're Undead to Me')

The Vampire Diaries does a lot of things well, but what really sets the show apart is its willingness to reach out to the fans. Most of the cast (really, only Steven R. McQueen excepting) are active users of Twitter along with the majority of the writers, directors and producers right the way down to the lowliest assistant. Who knew that 140 characters could reveal so much?

Ian is already the most familiar with keeping in touch with his fans: via his old website and his short interview segment the Friday Five in the early days. It's only natural now that he has turned to Twitter to share his thoughts – and to gain support for his many varied causes from any of his 685,000 followers (at the time of publication, the number grows daily!). 'By virtue of the use of social media and networking, there's been a paradigm shift and we are able to transfer a thought, whether it's a link or something a pop culture icon has done. That information exchange happens in such an expedient manner that it's frightening,' Somerhalder told conference-goers at *The Washington Post's* 'Energy is Urgent' Forum on 23 September, 2010. He also likes to use Twitter to create awareness – there are so many issues that he knows teens care about, such as the environment or bullying, but they simply don't have access to the right information. They want to help, but they don't know where to turn. Ian knows he can find those people on Twitter, and by making his tweets almost 50 per cent about his important causes and 50 per cent *The Vampire Diaries*, he's keeping his fans informed as well as entertained.

For other actors, like Zach Roerig (Matt Donovan), Twitter is just the simple, modern alternative to traditional fan letters: 'I have been horrible with fan mail my entire career. I think you really have to be diligent about it and stay on it, and I never was. With Twitter, it's so easy: I can see what the fans are saying. Should I choose to comment on it, I can, and I feel like it's the easiest way for me to contact the fans.' And a lot of fans have been able to get in touch with their favourite star just by tweeting them. One lucky fan did just that with Katerina Graham. An aspiring young journalist named Kaylie Rodrigues tweeted Kat to ask if she could interview her for her school newspaper. To her surprise, Kat said yes and a few days later, Kat called Kaylie personally to answer a few questions over the phone. It's that kind of amazing accessibility and down-to-earth nature of the stars of *The Vampire Diaries* that really sets them apart.

It's not just the stars, though. When Marcos Siega, director of the pilot episode (among many others) wanted to know what music to feature in the pilot episode of *The Vampire Diaries*, he thought, who better to ask what fans want to hear

The cast from the *Young Americans* TV show, including (*left to right*), Katherine Moennig, Ian, Rodney Scott, Kate Bosworth and Mark Famiglietti.

Above: Ian played Boone Carlyle in the first three series of epic TV show *Lost*. His character had a troubled relationship with half-sister Shannon (Maggie Grace, pictured).

Below: Ian with the cast of *Lost* at the Screen Actors Guild Awards in 2006.

Above: Ian starred as Dexter McCarthy alongside Kristen Bell in *Pulse* (2006)...

Below: ...before landing the role of Damon Salvatore in *The Vampire Diaries* alongside Paul and Nina Dobrev.

Above: One of Paul's earliest breakthrough roles was in the TV mini-series *Fallen*, where he played half human half angel, Aaron Corbett (2007).

Right: He also starred alongside Torrey DeVitto in comedy horror film *Killer Movie* in 2008.

Paul stars alongside Nina Dobrev in *The Vampire Diaries* where he plays vampire Stefan Salvatore.

Above: Paul poses for photos with Stephen Moyer and Kellan Lutz at *Cosmopolitan* Magazine's Fun Fearless Males of 2010.

Below: Paul, Ian and Nina say 'hi' to fans in London.

than the fans themselves? And so he went to Twitter to ask for music selections and that's how the show ended up with such great and diverse band tracks as White Lies, One Republic and Katy Perry.

At the PaleyFest conference, Julie Plec and Kevin Williamson told shocked tweeters that every Thursday, at 5pm, *The Vampire Diaries'* writing team in Los Angeles logs on to read live tweets streaming in as the episode airs on the East Coast of the US, in cities such as New York and Atlanta, where the cast is based. They love to gauge the fan reaction and it helps them to know that people out there appreciate their work. On occasion the writers will 'live tweet' an episode, offering extra tidbits of insight into certain scenes or lines of dialogue. Sometimes they inadvertently let slip information they didn't even realise the fans would care about – for example, when Julie Plec wrote that the writing team were in their local IHOP (International House of Pancakes) restaurant. Suddenly, they had loads of fans asking, 'Why IHOP?' Julie wrote back saying that it had to be IHOP – they sometimes needed a restaurant with 'a good Diet Coke mix and free refills' to get the writing juices flowing. Oh, the simple things in life!

That level of attention to detail from the fans made both cast and crew even more aware of how closely their tweets were watched. 'You have to think about what you're saying, because a lot of people are getting the message,' said Nina Dobrev. Over 650,000 people in her case! It actually took a little time for Nina's account to become 'verified' by Twitter and she had to post a picture of herself holding up a sign with her twitter name (standing next to Ian and his own twitter sign) to prove she was the real deal. There were (and still are) lots of pretenders online, who like to steal the identities of celebrities and put their integrity in jeopardy. If you want to find out whether it's really your fave celeb on Twitter, make sure to look for the little blue tick mark and the words 'Verified Account' above the username.

One of the last cast members to come to Twitter was Paul Wesley. Throughout the entire first season, he refused to sign up for an account despite the fact that his cast-mates Ian and Nina already had hundreds of thousands of followers. He mused on video to CW Source about his reluctance: 'Twitter… if I ever really need to say something and I really need to vocalise it to a large amount of people, maybe then I will get Twitter, maybe I'll just save it for something really special. Otherwise I can't really find any reason for it. I'm a really boring guy.' The 'boring' part is something that lots of his fans will surely not agree with, but it's taken a lot for the very private Paul to open up. Now that he has though, he's getting a lot of love for it. He only joined on 14 March 2011, but just a week later and he had over 100,000 followers. Paul's still got a long way to go to catch Nina and Ian, but he'll do so one day!

Want to follow *The Vampire Diaries'* cast and crew on Twitter? The main accounts are listed below so come in and join the conversation!

Crew

Kevin Williamson (Executive Producer/Writer) @kevwilliamson
Julie Plec (Executive Producer/Writer) @julieplec
Marcos Siega (Director) @msiega

Cast

Ian Somerhalder (Damon Salvatore) @iansomerhalder
Paul Wesley (Stefan Salvatore) @paulwesley
Nina Dobrev (Elena Gilbert) @ninadobrev
Michael Trevino (Tyler Lockwood) @M_Trevino
Joseph Morgan (Klaus) @_josephmorgan
Sara Canning (Aunt Jenna Sommers) @saradjcanning
Candice Accola (Caroline Forbes) @CandiceAccola
Katerina Graham (Bonnie Bennet) @KatGraham
Zach Roerig (Matt Donovan) @zach_roerig (previously @zgeorge222)

Other

Ian Somerhalder Foundation @IS_Foundation

Epilogue

You wake up back in your bedroom, and you're all alone. Have you been dreaming? Memory is foggy; time seems to have slipped past without your noticing... weren't you just in a graveyard?

You feel different, changed. Stepping out of bed, you pass by the mirror on your dressing table. Wait a moment, what's that on your neck?

There are two dark, blood-red puncture wounds in the curve just under your jawline and above your collarbone, perfectly positioned to access your carotid artery. He's left you alive... this time.

Damon was here, after all.

Blood Brothers

Blood Brothers

THE BIOGRAPHY OF *THE VAMPIRE DIARIES*' PAUL WESLEY

AMY RICKMAN

JOHN BLAKE

Published by John Blake Publishing Ltd,
3 Bramber Court, 2 Bramber Road,
London W14 9PB, England

www.johnblakepublishing.co.uk

www.facebook.com/Johnblakepub facebook
twitter.com/johnblakepub twitter

First published in paperback in 2011

ISBN: 978 1 84358 410 0

British Library Cataloguing-in-Publication Data:

A catalogue record for this book is available from the British Library.

Design by www.envydesign.co.uk

Printed in Great Britain by CPI Bookmarque, CR0 4TD

1 3 5 7 9 10 8 6 4 2

Papers used by John Blake Publishing are natural, recyclable products made from wood grown in sustainable forests. The manufacturing processes conform to the environmental regulations of the country of origin.

Contents

Spoiler Alert!

Hi, *The Vampire Diaries*' fans!

I've paid extra attention to make sure that you aren't spoiled for Season Two but if you haven't watched Season One yet, what are you waiting for? There are two delicious brothers just dying for your blood!

Paul Wesley

*

Stefan Salvatore

Introduction

Stefan: For over a century, I've lived in secret. Hiding in the shadows, alone in the world. Until now. I'm a vampire and this is my story. (1.01, 'Pilot')

The mist is rising. Somewhere, close by, a raven caws. A slow chill begins to creep up your spine – whether from the chill in the air or the eeriness of the scene, you're not sure. It occurs to you that a midnight stroll through a graveyard might not have been such a good idea. It's difficult to hear anything over the beating of your own heart. Did something just move in the shadows?

You feel the sudden heat of breath on your shoulder. Now you remember why you came here, to this place, to this graveyard with its broken tombstones and creeping vines. You came for one of the brothers. But which one will it be?

You spin around and out of nowhere, one of them has appeared. Tonight, it's Stefan Salvatore.

You breathe a sigh of relief: Stefan would never hurt you and

there's something about those hazel-green eyes that makes you feel like you're about to melt on the spot. There's wisdom in those eyes – wisdom, and pain. You must know more about this tortured individual. And luckily for you, Stefan has meticulously recorded all aspects of his life in hundreds of well-worn leather journals.

All you have to do is open one up and turn the page…

Chapter One

Family Guy

Stefan: We choose our own path. Our values and our actions? They define who we are. (1.07, 'Haunted')

When Paul Wesley walks into a room, he can't help but turn heads. With thicker, wavier hair than Robert Pattinson, a killer body and deep-set, soulful eyes that would be enough to melt any heart, his mere physical presence commands attention. But even with natural-born confidence and the world at his feet, Paul always gives off the impression he can't quite believe his own success. One thing is for certain – he definitely can't believe the attention his hair gets. It's the one thing almost every fan comments on, but it's also the one thing he has little to no control over – how he wears his hair is set out for him by *The Vampire Diaries*' stylists: 'I wasn't aware how long it had gotten till I watched the show. I was like, "Jesus Christ, my hair is ridiculous!"… I've been wearing hats!'

It's this self-deprecating sense of humour that he brings to

every interview and fan meet-and-greet that makes him instantly likeable. He's down-to-earth; he definitely hasn't allowed Hollywood to go to his head and even with just a quick glance at his past, it's easy to see where he gets his modest attitude. He comes from a close-knit family and had a grounded upbringing – one that instilled in him the importance of family, culture and heritage.

He was born Paul Thomas Wasilewski in New Brunswick, New Jersey, USA on 23 July 1982. New Brunswick, NJ is a small city with a history of producing big acting heavyweights – alongside Paul it is also the birthplace of multiple Academy Award-winning actor Michael Douglas of *Wall Street* fame and husband to Welsh actress Catherine Zeta-Jones.

Paul's parents, Agnieszka and Thomas Wasilewski, moved to the United States from Warsaw, Poland, just before he was born. They already had an older daughter, Monika Emara, and soon followed Paul with two young sisters: Julia and Leah. Growing up with Polish immigrant parents was hard on Paul, who often wished he could feel just like a regular American kid. 'I remember thinking, "I wish we could just be American, and drink soda and watch baseball,"' he admitted to *Watch* magazine. 'Of course, as you get older, you realise how cool it was to be different.'

It wasn't that his parents were altogether unfamiliar with America either: his dad was a computer engineer who did his training in New York's Chicago and Columbia University and his mum was a psychologist, although she stopped practising to look after her family. But even when they made the decision to move to the US permanently, his parents were determined that Paul and his sisters should not lose their Polish heritage. They encouraged them to be proud of their backgrounds and to learn their native language. In order to become fluent in Polish,

Paul spent four months out of every year in Warsaw, Poland, living with his grandparents, until he was sixteen. He still maintains a close relationship with his Polish relatives now, even though his schedule means it's much more difficult to get over to see them.

By far his closest relative is his grandfather and Paul makes sure they talk on Skype, in Polish, whenever he gets a spare moment. His grandparents are his greatest role models and it is partly their relationship that inspires his character Stefan's love for Elena: '[Stefan] is surely the most romantic character I've ever played. I believe in true love as well – I know it exists because I saw it. My grandparents have taught it to me by example; they have been together since they were sixteen.'

Before Paul went to elementary school, the Wasilewski family was on the move again – this time only a few miles away, to Marlboro, New Jersey, a town known for its good schools and impeccable safety record. But what Paul finds funny is that his hometown – and his state – has gained considerable notoriety, thanks to one specific reality TV show. On a late night television interview with host George Lopez, he experienced the power of *Jersey Shore*: 'I say I'm from Jersey and nobody applauds, and then we hear *Jersey Shore* and there's a huge applause,' Paul laughed. 'That is what the State of New Jersey has become.'

The cast of *Jersey Shore* wouldn't have been the type of people that Paul hung out with! He has never been comfortable with conformity and he was always a serious child, obsessed with analysing people and things. First and foremost, he loved his family and enjoyed nothing more than coming home to his mother's home-cooked cannelloni (was it fate that his most famous character would be of Italian descent?). He was extremely close to his sisters who used to tease him about his

slightly OCD tendencies: 'I have little OCD quirks and my family totally exploits them. Like, if I'm listening to the radio and someone puts the volume on the number 13, I have a minor panic attack. My little sisters love to do that to mess with me.'

Such an obsession is why the darker, more complicated aspects of Stefan appeal to him so much and this mindset can be traced back to elementary school days. He was the kind of child who needed a creative outlet – he just hadn't found the right one yet. At least, not until the third grade, when he 'got forced to do a school play because we all had to. They put me in a *Phantom* [*of the Opera*] mask and I was miserable at first.' (That sounds a bit of an understatement as Paul has also told *Women's Wear Daily* that he 'hated and resented it.') 'But then I kind of fell in love with it and ended up being, I guess, according to the teacher, pretty good at it,' he told the *Chicago Tribune*. He then found himself cast in every single elementary school play after that. In the summer of third grade, he enrolled in an arts program in New Jersey: 'I realised that I really enjoyed [acting].'

But this was a passion that was to cause almost as much trouble for Paul as it gave him pleasure: 'No matter how academic I was, no matter how much my father stressed studies, I always gravitated toward the arts because to me – you can read as many textbooks as you like – but to me life is about observing people and understanding things and nature. And art to me captures all that. It's just invaluable, and I can't imagine doing anything else.'

Not all of his schools were quite so understanding as his elementary school, though. He first started at the Christian Brothers Academy and didn't get on well there at all. In fact, the intolerance went both ways – he was eventually kicked out of the school halfway through completing high school diploma.

'I was a little bit of a troublemaker,' he admits, but 'not in a malicious way.' At the Christian Brothers Academy, where the focus was on sports and academics, he felt his passion for theatre was not socially acceptable. Indeed, it was certainly not considered cool to be into acting and the arts: 'I grew up in this town where we all put on this front; we all wanted to be tough. And acting wasn't necessarily cool. It was kind of something I embraced the hell out of, but then I'd come home and try to be Mister Tough Guy.' The Academy also had a particularly rigid set of rules and a strict uniform code that Paul, a born non-conformist if ever there was one, just couldn't abide. He loved ice hockey and used to play on the school team to let off steam but once he got kicked off the hockey side, he knew there was nothing left for him at that school: 'I was with a bunch of jock-y, racist kids. I thought, "This is an expensive school. My parents paid a lot of money [for me to attend]." And I got into a fight every day – it was just like this weird atmosphere.

'And they finally kicked me out, and I was really depressed about it. And then later it dawned upon me that, thank God, I didn't fit in with those kids because I don't want to be anything like those kids. So that's when I realised it was OK to sort of do my own thing. That's kind of like when I found a safe haven in acting – I think it may have been a catalyst.'

There might have been another catalyst too, however: Christian Brothers Academy was a private, all-boys school. No girls allowed. 'So how could you not get in trouble?' Paul pondered. 'There were no women – what were you supposed to do? So they generally had enough of my frequent trouble-making.'

Girls have always been important to Paul and as we have already seen, he is a born romantic. He experienced his first kiss

when he was 'nine years old and I was in a swimming pool. There was a girl there, and she dared me or I dared her into kissing me underwater. That wasn't a French kiss – that was like a "muah" kiss,' he told *Seventeen* magazine.

Another one of his favourite stories to share in interviews happened on Valentine's Day when he was fourteen years old. Eager to impress his girl crush, he stole his dad's credit card and proceeded to order the biggest, most obnoxious bouquet of flowers he could find in a catalogue, complete with a huge, cuddly teddy bear, but things didn't exactly go to plan. Although he asked for the present to be delivered anonymously, the company accidentally put his father's name, Thomas Wasilewski, on the 'From' card. The girl's parents were understandably disturbed – after all, why would a grown man be sending their daughter a huge bouquet on Valentine's Day? They called the Wasilewskis and Paul was forced to fess up as the sender. Not quite so romantic as planned!

Not romantic, maybe, but it was pretty theatrical. And very soon Paul would be able to demonstrate his acting flair beyond young love drama and elementary school plays.

Chapter Two

Soap Star

Stefan: I had a plan. I wanted to change who I was. Give my life to someone new. Someone without the past. Without the pain. Someone alive. (1.01, 'Pilot')

For most aspiring actors, breaking into the industry is a long, hard journey filled with disappointment, but for others it can seem more like an accident or a lucky fluke. For Paul, it was something in between. He knew he loved acting and he was a natural on set. As a child, he starred in a few television commercials, including one for the theme park, Great Adventure: 'I had to ride a roller coaster 14 times in a row – I vomited at the end,' he remembers. But it's still a big jump from screaming your lungs out in a commercial to earning a serious living. For that to happen, he needed an agent.

They can sometimes seem like worlds apart but New Jersey and New York City are actually only separated by a small stretch of water and even though he lived just an hour south of Manhattan, at first Paul didn't take his acting dream seriously.

He even thought he might try to play a professional sport: 'I played ice hockey obsessively for 14 years of my life,' he said, and even competing in the NHL (National Hockey League) seemed like a more realistic dream than acting (Paul has been spied at many a New York Rangers ice-hockey game – maybe reminiscing about what might have been?). But with the encouragement of his parents, 15-year-old Paul went to New York City and decided that modelling might be the best way into the industry. And it worked – right away, his gorgeous looks landed him a two-year-long contract with the world-renowned Ford Modeling Agency (Ford seems to be a magnet for the model-turned-actor-turned-vampire set as Ian Somerhalder and Kellan Lutz from *Twilight* were also clients).

However, Paul never really allowed modelling to sidetrack him from acting and he would travel up to New York by train on his own to attend improv (improvisation) workshops to brush up on his skill. He took part in every model and acting showcase he could find and that persistence paid off – only a short time later and he had landed himself an acting agent (Mike Jelline of International Creative Management). Paul then spent lots of time running back and forth to Manhattan for auditions and castings – casting directors were suddenly keen on this new young man on the scene. He might have been only fifteen then, but the doors to the acting world were about to be thrown wide open.

One of the best training grounds for actors are soap operas but funnily enough, Paul had never really heard of them before he got cast in one: 'I was fifteen or sixteen, auditioning for a soap opera. I didn't even know what a soap opera was. All I cared about was living in Manhattan and finding a way to not go to high school every day.' But soap operas are a common starting point in the industry as the turnover of roles is very

high. It's not surprising then that Paul's first proper acting job, when he was fifteen, was in a soap called *Another World*. He played a character called Sean McKinnon, 'but the show got cancelled the minute I joined the cast,' he told *Soap Opera Digest*. Luckily, Paul was picked up right away for the popular soap *Guiding Light*, as Max Nickerson, opposite Brittany Snow (*Hairspray* [2007]).

Guiding Light is in the *Guinness Book of World Records* as the longest-running drama in television and radio history, having broadcast from 1937 until 2009. Created by Irna Phillips, the show started out on the radio in 1937 before moving to TV in 1952. It has launched many famous actors' and actresses' careers, talents such as Christopher Walken, Kevin Bacon (*Footloose*), Hayden Panettiere (the cheerleader from *Heroes*) and Michelle Forbes (*True Blood*). It's a pretty impressive pedigree for any budding actor to start out with.

Paul wasn't the first person to star in the role of Max Nickerson. 'Max Nickerson #1' was originally played by an actor named Jesse Soffer but he was SORAS'd out of the role to make way for Paul. (SORAS'd is soap-speak for 'Soap Opera Rapid Aging Syndrome', where a character mysteriously disappears and then returns much older, even though only a small amount of 'real time' has passed.) The character of Max was a troubled teen, in and out of juvenile prison. Little did Paul know, learning to play the role convincingly would set him up for all his major parts yet to come…

Even though he only starred in six episodes of the soap, it proved to be the best acting education he could hope for. 'Soaps are such amazing training. *Guiding Light* allowed me to be comfortable in front of the camera and really learn my lines; it prepared me for the future,' he gushed.

'I would show up on set, this naive young kid, and would be

so intimidated by everybody who had been doing the show for so long.' He might have been intimidated, but he also made good friends on the show, some of whom he would work with in later life. 'One of my best friends in the world is Paulo Benedeti [who played Jesse Blue on the show]. He took me in and became like my older brother. I looked up to him so much. He had this really cool apartment in New York, and he'd invite me to hang out with him and his friends. I don't know why he wanted to hang out with me 'cause I was like this dorky kid. It was surreal.'

It's hard to imagine a guy as good-looking and confident as Paul ever feeling like a dork, but the very nature of his acting career made him feel isolated from fellow high-school classmates. At first, it was really fun for Paul. He was no longer at Christian Brothers Academy and had enrolled at a public high school – Marlboro High – instead. 'I was in high school and all my buddies had all these crap jobs. I felt like I was in *Big* [the film starring Tom Hanks about a kid who one day wakes up in an adult's body]. I was going into the city all by myself. I had this cool, adult job, and I was getting paid. It was just so amazing being in New York.

'I wasn't some weird loner in school,' he told *Teen Vogue*, 'but I definitely wasn't invited to any of the cool parties. Girls didn't like me that much – I didn't even go to my prom.' One girl liked him enough, though, as he stayed true to that girlfriend consistently throughout high school.

Paul couldn't seem to stay faithful to the same school, however. Having already transferred once after being expelled, he again found himself booted from school – this time from Marlboro High. His steady acting gig on *Guiding Light* meant frequent interruptions to the regular schooling week and Marlboro High just wasn't prepared to be as supportive as he

needed. 'I got kicked out of Marlboro High School because they couldn't tolerate the way I was missing school,' he explained. It wasn't just schools that he got kicked out of, either. Apart from his modelling/acting work, his first job was as a camp counsellor and he was fired after a month of doing that, too!

What Paul needed was a place that would acknowledge his burgeoning acting career and foster it. That establishment turned out to be Lakewood Prep in Howell, New Jersey (now known as Monmouth Academy). Even so, he never really felt as if he received the true American high-school experience. 'I never really got to establish my clique,' he admits. 'There were always so many cliques and I never really felt into a group, which isn't necessarily a bad thing – I actually recommend it.'

Clique or no clique, Paul is extremely grateful to Lakewood for their support: 'I would go to school once or twice a week, but they were really awesome and let me do the work from home. They facilitated it so I was able to get a high-school degree.' And after a rocky relationship with education, he graduated with his high school diploma in 2000. His high-school experience wasn't without its embarrassing moments, though. Paul described one of those red-faced times to iesb.com: 'I grew up in Jersey and I really thought it was cool to be a Homie G because we all wanted to be like rappers. So, I'd wear my pants below my ass and go walking down the hallway in high school and my pants literally fell off and I fell on my ass, and everybody saw it. I deserved it. I was an idiot. I should have pulled up my damn pants.'

Luckily for Paul, that's not how he'll be remembered! Thomas Costello, headmaster of Monmouth Academy, said: 'We're proud of Paul and we're proud of all of our graduates. They're all destined to do great things.'

Having finally secured his high-school diploma, Paul went on to try college too, at Rutgers in New Jersey, but unsurprisingly, it wasn't for him. He didn't want to waste his hard-earned money on a college education that he wasn't fully passionate about, or committed to. 'It was such a hard decision for me,' said Paul, on leaving Rutgers without completing a degree.

And so, with the full support of his family, he decided to make a go of acting full time. He was already financially independent as soon as he graduated and he bought himself an apartment in New York on his earnings from *Guiding Light.* 'I'm the No. 1 supporter of following your passion,' said Paul's mother, Agnieszka Wasilewski, absolutely beaming with pride for her son. 'I believe that if you have something that you really want to do, I'm not going to tell you that you have to stay in school first. He can always go back to school. I want to be proud of him, which I already am, but my only wish is for him to be happy.'

Chapter Three

Bit Parts and Big Breaks

Stefan: Yes, being a 150-year-old teenager has been the height of my happiness. (1.04, 'Family Ties')

It may seem as if Paul has had an easy rise in the acting world, but like any artist he's suffered his fair share of setbacks too. It was always his dream to make it big, but for that he needed the right breakout role and the right show to launch from. And while the roles were plentiful, nothing really seemed to stick.

Almost straight after making the decision to leave college for good, he landed a role in a television series called *Wolf Lake* (2001–02). It was a show that seemed to pre-empt the supernatural trend, as Paul was to play Luke Cates, a werewolf who was one of a pack wreaking havoc in the suburbs around Seattle, Washington. Playing a werewolf really appealed to his rebellious side: 'I always associate werewolves with this kind of instinctive anger. More like animals with rabies. When I was playing the werewolf, I was like 18 years old and I think I was

just like this teen who was running rampant. And I had a great time and it fitted the character perfectly, this alpha male machismo, and that was me,' he said. However, he didn't get to live out his alpha male persona for too long as the show was short-lived, with only nine episodes airing before it was cancelled. It had a real dark side too, with one reviewer calling it 'seriously disturbed and disturbing' (*Pop Matters*).

No matter, Paul had another role lined up in an instant. There was a lot of buzz surrounding this new show but it could have involved him making a huge, life-changing decision. If the show was to become as successful as he wanted, he would face seven years away from his family and a big move from New York City to Prague in the Czech Republic. 'I did the pilot for a show that shot in Prague, and if it had gotten picked up, I would have had to live there for seven years,' he told his local hometown newspaper, *Tri-Town News*. But the possibility of success was simply too tantalising. Paul knew he had to make sacrifices and this might be one of those times: 'I knew that if the show was that successful to be showing on NBC for seven years, that by the time I got back, I would be a well-known actor. So, I decided to do it.'

The show was *Young Arthur*, a period action-adventure series, and he was to play Lancelot, described in the NBC press release as 'a dashing French teenager'. The press release read thus:

> The year is 592. Welcome to the School of Glamorgan for young men. Bright, mischievous 16-year-old Arthur of Salisbury and his cocky older brother Kay have journeyed here through the dark and dangerous forests of England. Known for its harsh discipline as well as the large crocodile-filled moat that surrounds the school, Glamorgan is now home to young Arthur and his new

> roommate, a dashing French teenager by [the] name of Lancelot. Soon fast friends, Arthur and Lancelot meet sister and brother Morgana and Mordred, on whose vast land dwells the adjacent Girl's School.
>
> Arthur also finds himself vexed by a mysterious, sinister warrior named Lord Vortigen. But Arthur has destiny on his side (though he doesn't know it), along with a magical wizard who will soon reveal himself to be Merlin. It is Merlin who has come from the future to battle arch-nemesis Lord Vortigen to determine the fate of the 'future King of England.'

But although shows like *Merlin*, based on the Arthurian legend, are extremely popular now, back in 2002 it just wasn't the right timing again for Paul. The pilot didn't entice the network to pick up the series and he was now at a loose end.

The pilot might not have been shown to a public audience, but the TV and film worlds were certainly watching and it was clear to them that Paul Wasilewski was destined to be a star. At least one pair of eyes came from the set of *American Dreams*, a TV show set in 1960s America that followed one family as they dealt with the varied issues of the day: racism, adolescent rebellion, feminism. Paul's role was particularly nasty, as he was asked to play Tommy DeFelice, a macho football player with a serious racist streak: 'The producers of *American Dreams* saw the show in Prague [*Young Arthur*] and asked me to read for them,' he recalled, 'and I ended up on the show.'

He might have been on the show, but he still didn't have a leading role. Even as he flitted from show to show – his acting résumé shows stints at *Law & Order: Criminal Intent*, *The O.C.*, and *8 Simple Rules… for Dating My Teenage Daughter* – he still hadn't quite found the right platform. Sometimes these bit

parts worked in his favour – after all, any publicity is good publicity and getting his face out there and recognised was extremely important in the build-up to his career. Probably his favourite role was in *8 Simple Rules*, purely because it was his first sitcom and enabled him to showcase his comedic side. 'If [people are] a fan of *The Vampire Diaries* and they haven't seen me in anything else or know me, they probably don't know that I am the jokester. I like to kid around and I love comedy. I love to laugh and do impressions. I'm not great at it, but I like to make an ass out of myself,' he said. 'I did *8 Simple Rules... for Dating My Teenage Daughter* and I almost peed myself out of nervous energy. I have a good time when I feel safe and comfortable on set, with my family. When I'm on a live sitcom stage and there's 300 people waiting for me to make a joke, I just freeze up and act like an idiot – I love live theatre.'

One role that really helped boost his profile (despite him only appearing in one episode) was playing Lex Luthor's long-lost brother Lucas Luthor in *Smallville*. 'I have gotten more exposure from that one episode than any other,' he admits. 'It's crazy. I [went] to London for a *Smallville* convention. People really are huge fans of the show and my last name was Luthor, so it's bigger than just being a guest star. I'm the half-brother of Lex Luthor, which is a big deal.'

Even his next longest run, nine episodes in *Everwood* as Amy Abbott's boyfriend Tommy Callahan, was not to last although his character had a big impact on the show: '*Everwood* was the biggest, commitment-wise. I did a huge [story] arc, shooting up in Utah. I became really good friends with Emily VanCamp [who played Amy]. She's one of my best friends, we talk all the time. I also really loved shooting in Utah because I'm a huge snowboarder.' Like his *Smallville* character, Tommy Callahan was another bad boy – a drug dealer. Paul seemed to be

typecast into the bad-boy role. He loves playing them, however, and when asked whether he liked his character, Lucas Luthor, he said: 'Even though Lucas did things that were probably not the nicest things in the world, he had his own justification in his mind. It is up to the audience to decide whether or not they want to sympathise and have compassion for Lucas or if they think he's completely arrogant. I can't be biased toward my own character. As Paul the actor, Lucas is a good guy but I'd say that about any character I played that did something bad. There's always denial.'

His acting experience was by no means restricted to television, though. He also had bit parts in several movies ranging from small Indies to huge Hollywood blockbusters. On his résumé, you can spot *Minority Report* (2002) with Tom Cruise, *The Last Run* (2004), *Roll Bounce* (2005), *Cloud 9* (2006), *Peaceful Warrior* (2006) and *Killer Movie* (2008). And it was on the set of *Killer Movie* that he was to meet his future girlfriend, Torrey DeVitto – but more on her later.

He was earning a living with his craft, but it wasn't enough: Paul wanted to be more than just a jobbing actor. Besides, there were plenty of those around – newbies who showed up in LA every day who just didn't appreciate the art of acting the way he did. 'Acting is not something I take for granted, and I try to get better every day,' he told *Tri-Town News*. 'There's a lot of people in acting that aren't in it for the craft. They come out to LA expecting to get big, with no appreciation for the art.'

What he didn't realise then was that in order to succeed he had to switch things up a bit; he had to change his acting M.O. from bad boys back to supernatural beings. The problem was that Paul really didn't know much about the whole 'supernatural' genre: 'I don't know anything about comic books – I've never seen a *Star Wars* in my life, I'm literally clueless to

that genre. Not that this is like *Star Wars* but that whole sci-fi thing, I wasn't familiar with it at all.' Time to brush up on your fantasy, Paul!

Not only did he need to change the type of characters he was playing, but he had to change his name, too. Wasilewski was just too hard to pronounce and in any case, it didn't scream 'Make me a superstar'. So, in 2005, he got his family's permission and changed his name to the easier-on-the-tongue Wesley – and he hasn't looked back since.

He'd done the werewolf thing in *Wolf Lake*, but pre-*Twilight* (and a certain hottie named Taylor Lautner) werewolves were not particularly renowned for their attractiveness. Angels, on the other hand, now they could be hot – supernaturally so. It was the kind of role Paul was born to play.

Chapter Four

Angelology

Stefan: I don't want to survive… after what I've done,
it has to end. I just want it to be over. (1.20, 'Blood Brothers')

If Paul didn't already know that playing supernatural characters would lead to superstardom, then maybe he thought the secret to success was actually going to be young adult book adaptations. Before *The Vampire Diaries* was on his radar, his first leading role came in a television movie adaptation of a different popular young adult book series called *The Fallen* by Thomas E. Sniegoski.

The series follows a boy named Aaron Corbett, who finds out on his eighteenth birthday that he is a nephilim – half-human and half-angel. This explains some of the strange things that have been happening to him: for example, he wakes up suddenly able to speak every language in the world and he can also hear what his pet dog, Gabriel, is thinking. It also brings all sorts of trouble for Aaron as he's now pursued by the Powers

(angels who want to destroy him). With the help of two fallen angels, Zeke and Camael, Aaron realises that it might just be his destiny to redeem all of the fallen angels. His story continues through four books: *The Fallen*, *Leviathan*, *Aerie* and *Reckoning*.

These aren't your storybook angels and that's part of the series' appeal. Not being a huge fan of sci-fi, something else about the script appealed to Paul: 'The thing I like about this is that I think it's less sci-fi and more mythology. It's more historical, it's biblical in a way.' Thomas E. Sniegoski explained to *Innsmouth Free Press* where he got his story idea from – a painting on the ceiling of a church: 'The painting on the ceiling was of the Archangel Michael, with these gigantic wings, in full armour, sword – like a flaming sword raised above his head – and he was standing on the head of a man whose body slowly morphed into that of a serpent. And I looked at that for years and never really saw what it was that I was looking at. And then, one day, it was kind of like, "Wait a minute. That's an angel,"' he recalls.

'Now, in my mind, I'd been told my entire life, and seen my entire life, that angels were pretty ladies in nightgowns with big, cottony fluffy wings, or little babies in diapers and things like that. This was the first time that I had ever seen another interpretation and it really kind of almost just burned itself into my brain.'

It was a role that appealed to Paul the moment he heard about it. He immediately saw the potential in his character and it gave him an excuse to exercise his acting skills. Paul has always relished in method acting (a technique where an actor does his best to get into his character's head and experience the same emotions that his character is going through). His passion for acting really comes out when you hear him talk about it. For one role in particular, 'I literally forgot what I was doing while

I was reading my lines and was able to channel everything into the audition. I forgot where I was and literally felt like I had become this character, and it was just this incredible moment. Imagine being able to access that anytime.'

Playing a nephilim really gave Paul the opportunity to delve deep into his character and also to use a bit of creativity in developing his personality – something that isn't always possible when you play a normal human character. 'I enjoy the fact that [Aaron's] a social outcast and I really like the fact that we don't know much about his past,' he told *TeenMag*. 'He's never met his parents. There are so many interesting things to that – I thought it gave me a lot of range to play with. In the script it doesn't really tell you much about what happened to Aaron when he was in orphanages and stuff like that, it gave me the opportunity to make up my own stuff and create my own history for him. I really dug that.' He also got to show off his physical skills, learning how to sword fight (with a computer-enhanced flaming sword, at that) and how to act while constrained to a harness: 'I've had to train for shows before,' he said, 'but never like this. We did swords, we did kicks… I fly, like really fly in this.'

The television show had a very strange history. It was commissioned as a six-part mini-series, the first part being shown as a TV movie, *Fallen: The Beginning*, in 2006. Due to the ambitious nature of the show – and all the special effects that needed to be produced – fans had a long wait before they were able to learn the fate of Aaron and the fallen angels. A year later, the network – ABC – had scrapped the idea of the series but released two more episodes, *Fallen: The Journey* and *Fallen: The Destiny*, as mini-movies, each lasting 80 minutes.

But throughout the long wait for the final two episodes, the fans did have something else to keep them occupied. 'They're

launching a mythological online game, like *The Lost Experience*, that people can follow. It'll keep the audience hooked for a year. It's supposed to be pretty amazing,' explained Paul. And it *was* amazing, for the game won a Primetime Emmy award for Outstanding Creative Achievement in Interactive Television.

It was an experiment in the way people watch and interact with television shows. The target audience was young, tech-savvy and difficult to please; they needed something completely new and different to set the show apart from the millions of other teenage supernatural dramas that were springing up on networks across the US. The answer then was to keep the fans engaged with an ARG (Alternate Reality Game) based on the show.

Produced by Xenophile Media in Toronto, Canada, *Fallen: Alternate Reality Game* began with the launch of the *Fallen* website homepage, where an image of an oculus (a small, eye-like opening – like a round window) sat in the bottom corner. By clicking on the oculus, viewers were sent to a website 00112358.net (*The Da Vinci Code*-lovers and mathematicians will notice this is the beginning of the Fibonacci sequence), where a countdown awaited them. Once the countdown ran out, on 17 July 2006, the website opened up fully and the game began.

From there, fans set off on a hunt for a missing girl named Faith Arella – suspected of also being a nephilim, like Paul's character, Aaron. Using YouTube videos, 360° panorama photographs, e-mails, chat rooms, live events, multiple fictional websites, blogs and puzzles, fans gained access to a whole interactive universe surrounding the TV show. In total, the main website had over 2.8 million visitors and more than 250,000 people played the game – a massive success. The game ended four months later, in November 2006.

Needless to say, a lot of creative energy was going into the

show and Paul relished the opportunity to express more of his creative side as well. After the first movie aired in 2006, he said, 'the new executive producer and director have become friends of mine – I can't wait to sit down and give them my ideas. They've been so amazing, giving me creative freedom to change dialogue on the day. They've been incredibly accommodating.'

The second and third episodes aired on ABC on a special, *Fallen*-dedicated weekend in August 2007, following a re-showing of the first movie. Paul thought the final episodes were stronger: 'This is about twenty notches up; more serious, more mature. It's like *Batman Begins*. There's some amazing new characters and new actors. Bryan Cranston (*Malcolm in the Middle*, as Lucifer), Will Yun Lee (*Elektra*) and I'm really looking forward to everybody seeing it.'

Unfortunately for Paul, the show did not get brilliant reviews – even Sniegoski wanted to distance himself from it by the end: 'The very first movie, it's an OK translation of the first book. Not really. It's all right. It's not great [but] it's fun. I didn't mind it, it's fun. But the next two don't resemble the books at all, they just kind of did their own thing. But whatever. The check cleared, you know?'

Despite this, it was still a great learning experience for Paul in his first leading role. In order to really shine as a lead, you have to have a brilliant supporting cast and he learned so much from being able to train alongside experienced actors such as Tom Skerritt – best known for his role as Viper in *Top Gun* and for appearances in the television series *Brothers & Sisters*: 'He's such a great guy – we were so lucky to get him. I've seen some of his films and he's such a great actor. It's always an honour to work with someone who has a vast array of knowledge and experience.'

Although the television series was not to continue, the

author revealed for fans of the books that there might be a fifth one in the series called *The Fallen: End of Days.* This would pick up where the last book ended and hopefully launch a new series. And maybe now that Paul has become such a megawatt star, the TV series might get another outing, too.

Chapter Five

The Written Word

Anna: First rule about vampires? Don't believe anything you read. (1.17, 'Let the Right One In')

When *The Vampire Diaries*' TV series was first announced on 5 February 2009, the award for Most Commonly Used Phrase would have gone to: 'Our source material is 10 years older than *Twilight*!' It was the best retort they had to the constant accusations that they were just a Stephenie Meyer rip-off – if anything, they claimed, *Twilight* was taken from *The Vampire Diaries*! 'This actually came out before *Twilight*,' writer Kevin Williamson told *NewsOK*. 'The series of books is from 1990–91, so one would wonder if Stephenie Meyer read them.'

Of course, that wasn't true either. No one can deny the success of Meyer's books and the subsequent movies on their own merit – she managed to capture all the beauty and agony of teenage relationships, couched in a human-vampire love story. Yet it is an irrefutable fact that *The Vampire Diaries*' books

were published a decade before Meyer's *Twilight*. The key difference, however, is that *The Vampire Diaries*' series never quite attained the dizzying bestseller heights of *The Twilight Saga* – until now.

The author of *The Vampire Diaries*' series of books is L.J. Smith (the 'L.J.' stands for Lisa Jane). Born on 4 September 1965 in Orange County, California, Smith wanted to be a writer for as long as she can remember. Her talent with words was evident from an early age as an elementary school teacher praised her poetry, even though the ever-modest Smith said the poem was 'horrible'! However, those small words of praise were sufficient encouragement to give her the writing bug and she never really stopped pursuing her dream – even as she went on to study for a degree in Experimental Psychology at the University of California in Santa Barbara. Writing didn't really seem like a viable career at the time, so Smith started out as an elementary school and special education teacher to pay the bills. All the while, she was writing away.

Smith is famously slow at adopting technology (you'll read a story later about how she only bought a television so that she could watch *The Vampire Diaries*!) and she didn't own a typewriter or a computer. Therefore, she wrote her first book completely by hand and understood very little about the publishing process. She knew she had to get her manuscript typewritten, however, so she 'took [the] book to a professional typist and [the typist] got very excited about it. She said it was the best manuscript she'd seen, and she … asked if I was I interested in being agented. I was. Very. Of course, it still took some time to get the book sold – for one thing, I had to cut it by a hundred pages! But eventually Macmillan bought it, and my fate was decided. I loved writing and I knew I had to keep doing it.'

This first published book was called *The Night of the Solstice* (1987), which – along with its sequel, *Heart of Valor* (1990) – were the only two books she wrote for younger children (9 to 11-year-olds). She knew she would never stray too far from a young audience, though. Her reasoning is very simple – children's and young adults' books were the kind she read most! 'I knew the kind of books I liked to read and there just weren't enough of them. Nothing to do but write them myself,' she said. The books were well-reviewed but never really took off sales-wise.

Smith's writing skill was evident and she soon quit her job as a teacher to enable her to write full time. There was still that niggling issue of bills to pay though, and so when her publisher approached her with an idea for a trilogy of books, she leapt at the chance to write it.

The original concept for *The Vampire Diaries* was formed by the team at Alloy Entertainment led by Les Morgenstein, who desperately wanted a vampire-filled trilogy. Alloy Entertainment is a book packager, who have been very successful in developing concepts (or 'properties') and selling them on to publishers and television companies (among their successes are huge properties like *The Sisterhood of the Traveling Pants*, *Gossip Girl* and *Pretty Little Liars*). 'They wanted me, within nine months, to produce three books about vampires,' said Smith. 'So the idea was that there were two brothers who were both in love with the same girl: one good brother, one bad brother. And I kind of like the bad brother better, that's Damon, and he's one of my favourite characters to work with, so it didn't come out exactly perhaps as it was intended, but it seems that people enjoy the effect so I can't complain.' Those were prophetic words, as it would be L.J. Smith's love of Damon that would eventually end her association with *The Vampire Diaries*' series. Alloy went on to sell

the books to HarperCollins publishers in the US and Hodder in the UK.

Smith wanted her books to be as original as possible: 'I quickly read up on classical vampires and soon realised that I wanted *The Vampire Diaries* to be unlike any book that had been written before it – to have a *reluctant* vampire – one who didn't want to be a creature of darkness, but couldn't help his nature. So Stefan was born. When I added Elena and Damon to the mix I found I'd fallen in love with all three characters.' In the wake of *Twilight* – which features an entire family of reluctant vampires – this idea doesn't seem too original. But Smith really can be credited with bringing a teen-friendly pathos to the vampire myth that was missing in the previous generations of vampire books. Vamps have always been sexual creatures (in a predator way, like Dracula or Lestat), and sometimes romantic, but rarely have they been plagued with the kind of teen angst that Stefan (and eventually Edward) experiences.

Her vampires were real monsters however, with an inability to go out in the sun (except for those with special enchanted rings), pointed fangs and bloodthirsty natures. Some even had other powers such as shape shifting, super speed and strength. Yet she built some weaknesses into her vampires, too. Apart from not being able to sunbathe, they could be killed by a wooden stake through the heart, were unable to enter people's homes without being invited in and were weakened by a herb called vervain (also known as verbena). Smith took the theory that vervain could ward off evil spirits and witches from medieval European beliefs. It just goes to show how much research she put into the creation of the mythology behind *The Vampire Diaries* despite not having much time to write.

Smith has a curious theory as to why vampires are such popular monsters: 'I believe in the theory of redemption. I

think a lot of us want to believe that any of these gloriously-beautiful, inherently-chilling creatures of the darkness can get a little closer to the light through the love of a nice human girl.' Yet her stories are more than just the redemption of the vampires, who are inherently evil and must fight to be good; they also concern redemption for the human characters in the story, like Elena. 'The story is [about] how a girl who's really kind of a social butterfly and an egoist learns that she's not the [centre] of the universe; she's not the thing the world turns around. And she realises that other people mean a lot more than she does,' she told *Author Hour.* She also sees the vampire stories, especially the *Vampire Diaries* and *Twilight* kind, as being like roller coasters – you can be terrified of them, you can scream all the way through the ride but in the end you know that they're not going to kill you.

When they were finally published in 1991, it was a full 10 years before the first *True Blood* book by Charlaine Harris and 13 years prior to Stephenie Meyer's *Twilight*. The first three *Vampire Diaries* books (*The Awakening*, *The Struggle* and *The Fury*) were a moderate success, gaining legions of loyal fans who kept the series running but the books still didn't hit the bestseller lists or make any defining impact on the market.

As she wrote the first three books incredibly quickly, Smith wasn't about to rest on her laurels and set about writing more. She penned a fourth book in the *Vampire Diaries*' series called *Dark Reunion* (1992) and more trilogies – including *The Secret Circle* (1992), another fantasy romance series, but this time focusing on witches. Cassie, the main character from *The Secret Circle*, finds out that she is a witch (and descended from Salem witches just as Bonnie is in *The Vampire Diaries*' TV series, although not in the books) when she is sixteen years old. Again, Smith created a strong, female central character for the book, just

like Elena. She called these female protagonists her 'Velociraptor Sisterhood' – a group of smart, determined women not afraid to stand up for their fellow female friends. It was a strong message that she was trying to put forth: that it was OK to be brave and clever, yet still fall madly in love. Other trilogies followed, including *The Forbidden Game* (1994) and *Dark Visions* (1994–95). In 1996, she launched her biggest (in terms of number of novels) series to date – *Night World* – a series of 10 books about a secret society of supernatural races that must live among humans without their knowledge.

Smith is the kind of writer who needs to write to live – she just doesn't feel the same without a project. However, a string of personal tragedies in the late nineties meant that she was unable to find her muse for almost a decade: 'My brother-in-law had some very serious medical problems that frankly he was not supposed to live through and then my mother unfortunately passed away from lung cancer. So for 10 years actually, just like a faucet, my imagination was turned off and you can imagine what agony that is for a writer. I really wanted to write that whole time and was trying to, but I was not able to.'

Meanwhile, Smith hadn't realised that her books were enjoying a resurgence following the publication of *Twilight*. Her publishers had decided to repackage them with a sexier front cover to draw in the market that, post-*Twilight*, was screaming for still more vampires. 'I was busy nursing my mom, and I didn't know that they had republished my books until they were telling me that the second one had debuted at #5 on the *New York Times* Best-Seller List,' she told *MTV*. But the renewed success of her books came at a certain price, for Smith started to receive tons of mail, some of it vitriolic: 'There's two kinds of floods of mail I get. One, there's the floods of mail

from people accusing me of stealing and they list about 30 things from *Twilight*. I usually write back just one sentence: "Look at the copyright date." Actually, I get a tremendous amount of apologies back. A lot of people have the guts to write back and say, "Oh, my God, I'm so sorry."

'I have other people who are very incensed and want to write to me about all the things that *Twilight* has in it that were in both [my other supernatural series] *Night World* and *Vampire Diaries*. But I haven't seen *Twilight*. I haven't read any of the books. I can't really comment on any of that.'

For someone who has spent most of her life writing about the supernatural, Smith considers herself to be a very grounded and logical person, who was never religious or mystical. Everything changed, though, when her mother passed away. After that, Smith felt as if she had someone watching over her, to help get her out of her funk: 'It was my mom who did it. She came back, sat on my shoulder, and said, "Yes, you can write again." And I almost physically felt her presence, which is rather odd because I'm a very logical person.'

It was during this period that word came through her literary agent that *Vampire Diaries* had been optioned for the small screen. Smith was cautiously optimistic (when a book is optioned, this means that a film or television company has bought the rights to produce a screen-version of a story, but they are under no obligation to actually make the show or movie). She was well aware that books are optioned all the time and there are many stumbling blocks to jump over before any cameras start rolling. 'First you hear that maybe they'll do it; they take an option on it. So at every stage I just said, "Calm down, calm down. It's probably not going to happen." And now that they've just told me that they were doing a full season of filming, then I allowed myself to say,

"Yipee!"' she told Matthew Peterson on a radio show called *The Author Hour*.

Finding out that Kevin Williamson was attached to the project helped as well. 'I was so thrilled that it was Kevin Williamson who was doing this, you know, because it was just so exciting to get the guy who had done *Dawson's Creek* to be doing my work,' she admitted. Knowing he was on side gave her the confidence to know that her characters would be treated with respect, even if he did diverge from her original plotlines. (Which, of course, they did greatly – turn to the next chapter to read just how the show differs from the books.)

Naturally, she was full of nervous trepidation when the show came out – like any writer, she didn't want to see her characters and ideas butchered on the small screen. And at first, she wouldn't give her full endorsement to the series. After reading the script, she especially had a problem with the portrayal of drugs on the screen (in the first few episodes of the show, Elena's teen brother Jeremy deals painkillers to the girl he loves, Vicki). 'I suppose everyone must be allowed to have their own versions of the characters and the story. And if I can say that to readers then I can say that to the small gods of the TV pilot,' she wrote on her blog. She didn't even go to see the pilot, although she did get positive feedback from her agent.

It wasn't as if she could watch the show at home either – before *The Vampire Diaries*, Smith didn't even own a TV! 'I had to actually buy one and get the cable, and get the guy to come in and turn it on and all that,' she told *The Author Hour*.

Once she finally got around to watching the show, she supported it 100 per cent, though. On a Simon & Schuster blog tour (the publishers of her *Night World* books), Smith wrote: 'I think they're doing a great job of interpreting the books for a mainstream teen audience who just happen to like vampires. I

was scared myself about the drugs, but Elena is a champion against them and that is very important to me. I must admit I have some mixed feelings about the pilot, too, but the cinematography's great, the music is great, the character chemistry is great, the acting is (with one exception) great. And finally, PLEASE understand that I didn't make one of these changes. They were all made by Kevin [Williamson] and Les [Morgenstein] and Julie [Plec], and so please don't blame me. I am just another grunt who works here.'

With the success of *The Vampire Diaries*' show, Smith was asked to add more books to the series. In 2009, she released *Nightfall*, part of *The Return* trilogy, and followed up with the second book, *Shadow Souls*, in 2010. This time, the books were hugely successful on both sides of the Atlantic, even gaining spots on the *New York Times* and *Sunday Times* bestseller lists. This sparked a resurgence of interest in Smith's previous books, causing all her works from other series to be re-released with shiny new covers. HarperTeen capitalised on the popularity of the series by releasing prequels, known as *Stefan's Diaries*, which tied in to the television series mythology rather than the book series. Kevin Williamson and Julie Plec were consulted about the storylines, as well as L.J. Smith, and they were released in 2010–2011 (*Origins* was released on 2 November 2010, *Bloodlust* on 4 January 2011 and *The Craving* on 3 May 2011).

Yet, in early 2011, a controversy arose surrounding Smith that shook *The Vampire Diaries*' fans to their core. After the final book in *The Return* trilogy, *Midnight,* it was announced that Smith would no longer be writing *The Vampire Diaries*' books. Her name would be retained on the cover as author, but the new trilogy, *The Hunters*' series (*Phantom*, *Moonsong* and *Eternity*), would be ghostwritten. It was all because the publishers and Alloy wanted to see Stefan and Elena continue together, whereas

Smith – who has always preferred Damon to Stefan – saw Elena ending up with the older brother. Unable to get past this disagreement, writer and publisher decided to part ways.

But how could Smith be removed from her original project? This was only possible because of Alloy's position as a book packager. As they had come up with the original concept – i.e. the vampire brothers fighting over a teen girl – they owned the copyright to the story, despite L.J. Smith creating all the other elements to the book, such as the setting, characters and most of the plot. Fans were completely outraged and even threatened to boycott the series and HarperCollins products but Smith generously encouraged a more tempered reaction on her blog: 'Most importantly, I want to ask anyone who was thinking of it, not to boycott Harper's or anyone. It just doesn't make sense. Although I wanted and still want more than anything to be able to continue *The Vampire Diaries*' series myself, there's no point in not trying the new books. (And remember, for fans of Bonnie and Damon, and strict Stefan and Elena fans, the immediate dynamics may be more to your liking.) Besides which, *Midnight*, which is all mine, is coming out in March, and I believe there may be some of my writing in *Phantom*.'

Whether or not Smith is writing the next books, it is her legacy that lives on in the characters that she created.

Chapter Six

Books Versus Show

Damon: You can turn it off, like a button you can press. I mean, Stefan's different. He wants the whole human experience. He wants to feel every episode of *How I Met Your Mother*, so he shuts his feelings out. The problem is, as a vampire, your instinct is not to feel. Isobel chose the easier road – no guilt, no shame, no regret. I mean, come on, if you could turn it off, wouldn't you? (1.21, 'Isobel')

Whenever a book is turned into a screenplay – be that for a film or a television series – there will always be changes. For Kevin Williamson, seeing how a favourite book was interpreted onscreen was all part of the fun: 'When I was growing up, I was an avid reader and I read everything that was adapted into a movie or a TV show. And I always liked the surprises. I liked to see the changes.' Easy to say when you're not the author whose work is being altered! The main worry for L.J. Smith and for loyal fans of *The Vampire Diaries* books was whether the adaptation would be handled with respect and consideration, not just thrown together haphazardly with no attention to the original material. This was, of course, totally understandable to Williamson and his co-creator Julie Plec. 'We

want to do the books justice,' Kevin told the *LA Times*. 'We're going where the story takes us, but at the same time, we're really trying to honour the original books. Our main concern is to honour the tone of the books and the major themes. We want to honour the love story: the romance and the betrayal.'

Both were keen to point out that television and books are very different mediums, although they attempt to tell the same message. Twenty-two one-hour episodes are very different from a 250-page book. TV shows are even more likely to deviate from books than movies as the storylines have to progress on a very different timescale: 'I like to say that if you look at the gross content of the books, we're following it incredibly closely,' said Plec. 'But if you look at the timeline, it's varying quite a bit. We're telling some of the stories a lot faster, some of them a lot slower. But the core relationships are very specific, and very much what we're playing with. We've got about five books that we're hopefully turning into many, many seasons. The lead character in the books is actually dead by book three, she's a ghost. It might take us a bit longer to do that!'

Looking at the changes on paper, fans of Smith's original books were understandably concerned. In fact, the show was written so differently from the books, that Williamson and Plec advised the cast not to read them before shooting – a rule which, obviously, a few of them broke, including Paul Wesley. But Candice Accola, who plays one of Elena's best friends (who sometimes gets jealous of all the attention Elena gets), explained to *Star Pulse* why she *didn't* read Smith's series: 'At first I wanted to read the books, but after talking to the producers and the writers they are not sticking to it so much. We were kind of advised not to. I also didn't want to have a preconceived notion of who Caroline was when they were going to possibly write her in a different light. I opted

not to read the books so I could find out who Caroline was on my own.'

Accola, however, had it easy: her character, Caroline Forbes, didn't change too much from the book character (apart from her last name) and fans could get past that. Yet some changes were made that seemed completely arbitrary and one change in particular brewed into a cauldron of controversy that would become known as the 'Hair Affair'.

In the books, Elena is a bubbly, popular and blonde teenager – indeed, Smith makes frequent mention of her lustrous golden locks. In fact, Julie Plec thought they had probably lost the hardcore fans just by virtue of changing the main character's hair colour from blonde to brunette: 'There is a core fan-base for the books. And they're mad that the lead character is not blonde. So when you start there, there's not a lot you can do,' she told *The Torch* online.

Fortunately, by the time the series aired and Nina Dobrev had established herself in the part of Elena Gilbert, the fans could see why she had been cast in the role. Even Smith came round in the end: '[Elena] is both strong and gentle, and who cares if she's not blonde? I will go on writing her as a blonde goddess with a bit more edge, and the TV show will at least have some of my ideals…' she wrote on her Simon & Schuster blog.

As for Williamson and Plec, they had known that they needed to rewrite Elena's character a little bit because of the nature of their medium. They had to have a main character that they could grow and develop through the series and for that, they needed the perfect leading lady, who they found in Nina Dobrev. But they needed to alter her personality a bit, too: the Elena in the books is a sharp-edged mean girl, with none of the television Elena's sweetness. In fact, many of the book's fans

consider the TV-Elena to have the personality of the book character Meredith Sulez, book-Elena's best friend, who hasn't yet shown up in the television series (although Williamson and Plec have both said to expect her). 'We need a main character that people can relate to,' said Kevin. 'The Elena of the books was not it.'

For those fans missing Meredith, Julie stresses patience. 'Time, money and a lack of story at the beginning,' is how she explained Meredith's absence, in a Tweet no less! 'Plenty for her to do in the long run.'

Another somewhat arbitrary change was the background of the Salvatore brothers and of Bonnie, too. In the pilot script for the show, the brothers' last name had been changed to Whitmore. They changed it back to Salvatore before the series aired, however, much to the delight of the fans. In the books, the Salvatore brothers were from Florence, Italy, and were born (and turned into vampires) during the Renaissance period. This would make Stefan and Damon much older than 160 – can you imagine the wisdom Paul Wesley would have to dig deep to find in order to play a 400-year-old? The decision to change the brothers' backgrounds to be from American Civil War-era Mystic Falls, Virginia was controversial in Smith's eyes. 'It was felt that a typical teen audience wouldn't sympathise with Italians as well as Americans,' she wrote. 'I didn't and don't agree, but who am I? I'm listed as "Source" in the credits. The reason they made the boys Civil War-era guys was because there was so much all ready [sic] about Fell's Church of the Civil War (the high school name, the Cemetery, etc.) and if the guys are not Italian it made sense for them to have been from the same Civil War town.'

For Plec, the Civil War connection proved a bit of a sticking point. Although changing that particular part of the

Salvatore back-story took them further away from *Twilight* (some of whose characters, like the Volturi, are particularly tied to the Renaissance era Italy), it brought them dangerously close to *True Blood*, as the main vampire in that show – Bill Compton – is also a Confederate soldier turned at the end of the Civil War and the rest of the show features a lot of Civil War-era references. 'We didn't realise the *True Blood* comparison when we were doing it,' Julie admitted to *Soap Opera Weekly*. 'But for me, if I'm a teenager and I haven't read the books, or I'm a 22-year-old watching the show, there's just something very interesting about our own history that happened a lot more recently than the Renaissance. And, honestly, a 400-year-old vampire is just a little bit creepier than a 162-year-old vampire – as far as the "falling in love with an older man" thing goes.'

Regarding Bonnie, many fans were confused when they first saw the series. The Bonnie in the books is Bonnie McCullough, a red-headed, fair-skinned lass whose magic comes from her Druid ancestors. In the TV series, Bonnie is Bonnie Bennett, a young black teenage girl, who is descended from Salem witches. But the actress who plays Bonnie, Katerina Graham, knew there was more to her character than just her skin and hair colour: 'The character was written Bonnie McCullough and she was this redheaded, Irish-descended girl but she was also very small like me, and she was bubbly and funny and silly like me, so I'm like "Oh, it works. I can make this work just fine." We just have the hair and the skin tone a little different. Other than that, we're totally the same,' she told Fall TV. 'The most important thing is that you capture who these characters are – their personality, how they interact with the other characters.'

Some of the changes were led by the actors themselves. For

example, in the books the character of Katherine (Elena's evil vampire doppelgänger, who is responsible for turning Stefan and Damon into vampires) is the daughter of a German baron – giving her the last name von Swartzchild. She was turned in the early Renaissance period, probably around 1490. In the television series, she is Katherine Pierce, an American, but on the show Katherine's (and therefore, Elena's) ancestors are from Bulgaria – which is where Nina Dobrev hails from. Nina told Spoiler TV: 'In the books, Katherine comes from a German heritage. It may be because I'm Bulgarian, but I think we all agreed that Bulgaria has a sense of mystique that is strangely unique. Plus, it doesn't hurt that I already speak Bulgarian. The writers heard me speaking Bulgarian to my mom on the phone while I was on set one day. One thing led to the other and voilà!'

There were also plot devices in the story that simply weren't explained anywhere in the original books, which meant that Williamson and Plec had to invent back-stories where they saw gaps. Probably the biggest unanswered question of the book series was why Katherine and Elena look so much alike. Julie said: 'We were [asking each other], "Why do they look the same? What do the books say?" and the books don't say! At one point, Katherine looks at Elena and says, "We look awfully alike; we must be related somehow [and that's it]." This is what we're working with, so we have to stray from the paradigm to make good story.'

Sometimes changes were made for legal reasons – like the change from Fell's Church, Virginia (the books) to Mystic Falls, Virginia (TV show), which they had to make because they couldn't get clearance in time for 'Fell's Church'. Sometimes things just sounded better: the last name for Todd Lockwood sounded more 'old money' than Todd Smallwood in the eyes of

the network executives. Sometimes the television show introduced a little foreshadowing, for example by changing the school's football team name from 'Wildcats' to 'Timberwolves'. Regardless of why the changes were made, the scriptwriters were conscious that they weren't going to please everyone. 'The books still have very, very loyal fans of that franchise and the same way that we were afraid of being compared to *Twilight*, we were afraid of letting the book fans down,' Julie admitted. 'And I think there are probably quite a few out there who sort of said, "Eh, I don't like the way you guys did that." But I think more importantly there are so many of the die-hard book fans who have been very, very embracing of the path that we've taken.'

Most of the cast take a very Zen attitude to the changes. Ian Somerhalder was particularly laid-back and at the PaleyFest panel, he observed: 'Predictability is what we always live with and the antithesis of that is what makes things exciting, if that makes any sense at all.' What he means is that change is exciting! And in the case of a television series that could go on for many years versus a trilogy of books, the show is bound to deviate from the book plots even more.

Most important to Kevin Williamson was getting the tone of the show right. 'I want it always to be real,' he told *SFX*. 'We've tried to find a tone that fits somewhere between where we're emotionally invested and we care about those people, versus outlandish genre high jinks. We're caught in the middle and we try to have our cake and eat it but one of the things that attracted me to these stories was the mythology of the town. I think that's what L.J. Smith did really well, she created this sort of mythology that wherever blood was shed in an epic battle then that place attracts the paranormal.'

But Smith herself put it best: 'There is a big difference

between five books and a full-season TV show, and the spirit of the book is honoured throughout. The books and the TV show are just two different ways to tell a tale.'

Chapter Seven

One True Love

Anna: Well, well, Elena Gilbert. You really are Katherine's doppelgänger. You must have the Salvatore boys reeling.
(1.14, 'Fool Me Once')

Even with such incredible source material, for *The Vampire Diaries*' show to succeed they needed the best actors and actresses possible for the leading roles. And even before the hunt for the hot vampire men could start, Kevin Williamson and Julie Plec had to find the right leading lady.

Growing up, Nina Dobrev could only dream of becoming a Hollywood superstar but now, at the tender age of twenty-two, her dreams have finally started to become reality. Her grace and poise in the character of Elena Gilbert has won her critical acclaim and the love of the fans, and by taking on the dual role of Katherine Pierce, Nina has proved her versatility as an actress equally comfortable with playing the struggling single mum as the innocent girl-next-door or a conniving evil vampire. Williamson has nothing but praise for her: 'Aside from being

enormously gifted, what's so great about her is that I don't think she knows how talented she is. I predict Oscars for her,' he gushed to *TV Addict*.

It's hard to believe, then, that Nina almost didn't get the chance to audition for *The Vampire Diaries* as the network (The CW) already had a very specific actress in mind for the role. '[They] wanted us to hire Ashlee Simpson-Wentz [sister to singer Jessica Simpson]!' said co-executive producer and director Marcos Siega. Fortunately for Nina (and for us viewers!) Ashlee accepted a role in the remake of *Melrose Place*, which had a short-lived season in 2009–10.

Like Paul, Nina Konstantinova Dobreva grew up in a multinational household and speaks multiple languages, including English, French and Bulgarian. She was born on 9 January 1989, the second of two children in the capital city of Bulgaria, Sofia, but her parents sought to escape the communist country and move somewhere with more opportunity for their children to succeed. In the end, they decided on Canada and they moved to Toronto when Nina was only two years old. 'My parents literally started out with nothing,' she said. Her dad, a computer specialist, and her mother Michaela, an artist, were able to find work in Toronto and started building a life there for Nina and her older brother, Aleksander.

Nina is very close to her family. She gets her artistic side from her mum, who has a Masters in Fine Arts. Michaela worked as an art conservator and helped to preserve many of the valuable medieval collections held at the University of Toronto. She currently runs a company called Paint-a-World, which offers painting tours around some of the most beautiful parts of Europe. Nina is also close to her brother: 'I was the annoying little sister, who wanted to follow him everywhere and do everything he did,' she laughs.

But it wasn't for painting that Nina was beginning to find her passion. While attending the Wexford Collegiate School for the Arts, she discovered her love of acting, but she also realised that she had a talent for dance and gymnastics as well. It was a great way for her to express her creativity and also to expend some excess physical energy. In 2005, aged only sixteen, she represented Canada in the Aesthetic Group gymnastics World Championships. Aesthetic gymastics is an older form of rhythmic gymnastics, performed without the use of any props (such as ribbons or batons, which are common in rhythmic gymnastics). The routines are often very physically demanding, mixing dance with gymnastics and encouraging flowing, graceful movements that require a lot of skill to complete. Nina sums it up as 'synchronised swimming, only with gymastics'. 'I loved the competitive aspects, and I loved the physical and social aspects of it,' she told *Bayview* magazine. 'A lot of my friends were doing it, and it was fun: it was dancing, it was performing, but it was still a challenge. The training was really intense – anywhere from three to four hours, six days a week.'

She describes herself in high school as a very hard-working person, who pursued her goals with gusto: 'I wanted to be the jock, and I wanted to be a dancer and actress. I was also a gymnast and very academically driven. I always had a lot on my plate and was really overwhelmed. Not much has changed – I'm constantly trying to one-up myself and raising the stakes,' she told *Teen Vogue*. After high school, she began studying sociology at Ryerson University in Toronto but it wasn't for her – after all, all of her friends were going to university to discover what they wanted to do in life. Nina already knew what she wanted to do. She told an interviewer on AOL.com about the tough decision to break away from following the traditional path of high school–university–career: 'I love what

I'm doing,' she said, 'and I couldn't wish for anything better, but I'm also trying to go to university, in my first year, and I'm never there. People go to university to learn how to be what they want to be in life. I'm already doing it, so I'm conflicted.' She sensed herself becoming quickly burnt out. 'I wasn't able to do any of them [university, acting or dance] perfectly. I was just kind of mediocre. I was trying to divide myself in three ways, and each was suffering. I had to realise there is no such thing as perfect, but it took a couple of anxiety attacks to figure that out.'

What she really wanted to do was act. She dedicated herself to learning the craft first and enrolled at The Armstrong Acting Studios in Toronto, run by acting pro Dean Armstrong. 'The Armstrong Acting Studios helped prepare me for the industry in every aspect and through every step of the way; from finding an agent to auditioning to being on set. I learned the fundamentals of scene work (making strong choices, analysing and breaking down characters, etc.) and practise them on a regular basis,' said Nina in a testimonal on The Armstrong Studios' website. And she isn't the only famous face to have taken classes there – Miley Cyrus (*Hannah Montana*) also counts herself as one of Dean's students. Since she started at The Armstrong Studios when she was seventeen, Nina considers herself to be a slow bloomer in the acting world: 'I started in the business quite late compared to all my other friends. I was sixteen or seventeen and at first I went to Performing Arts High School in Toronto. I was always dancing and doing gymnastics and performing in different ways but it wasn't acting until I got an agent and started auditioning for movies and TV shows.'

With her stunning good looks, Nina couldn't help but draw the attention of both modelling and acting agencies. She

modelled for a while and also starred in television commercials before things started to fall into place: she auditioned for three different parts – and managed to land all three. This was where she would finally get to prove herself as more than just a pretty face.

The first job was as single mother Mia Jones in *Degrassi: The Next Generation*, a long-running Canadian teen soap opera. It was the perfect start for Nina, as it really allowed her to learn on the job. Funnily enough, she wasn't a huge fan of the show before joining the cast: 'I was of course familiar with the show and heard all the hype, but I didn't really watch it because I didn't have the time. Actually I am not the biggest TV person – I'm really into school, sports and gymnastics.' She did make sure to catch up on what she had missed out on quickly, though: 'I literally borrowed Seasons One through Five and watched them all back-to-back within a month.'

She was incredibly nervous about joining her first cast, especially one that had been around as long as *Degrassi*. What's more, she really credits the show with being able to keep her grounded while helping her improve and grow as an actor: 'The show taught me a lot about being on set and how to act on camera, because I was very green. I ended up spending four years on *Degrassi*, but because it was a Canadian show made far away from Hollywood, I was able to get into the business more progressively. A lot of people who start acting at an early age lose their sense of reality, but I had time to be a normal kid while at the same time doing this thing I loved.'

Playing a teen mom was really hard – especially as it was so far removed from her real high-school experience. Nina was always the responsible one, with her focus on sports, her studies and her art but she threw herself into the role and did a lot of research to make sure she could play Mia Jones authentically.

She told teen website Miss O and Friends: 'It was challenging because it's not me. I went to a lot of websites that dealt with teenage pregnancy; I read a lot of stories about girls having to go through what Mia did. There's the alienation factor and there are all the stories and rumours, having everybody judge you. It isn't easy.'

The second and third jobs were on the big screen – a film adaptation of Anne Michaels's novel *Fugitive Pieces* with Rosamund Pike (*Pride and Prejudice*) and Ayelet Zurer (*Angels & Demons*) and another film called *Away from Her* (2006), which was the directorial debut of the award-winning Canadian actress Sarah Polley. Nina was extremely independent by this point; although she had her parents' support, they didn't coddle her through the early stages of her career. 'I didn't have a stage mom at all,' she said. 'I was the one who planned out my auditions and drove myself an hour-and-a-half into the city.' Her persistence and determination was paying off for Nina was creating a stir in the Toronto acting scene. She caught the eye of a lot of big players in the Canadian film world, including director Atom Egoyan, who cast her in the erotic thriller *Chloe* (2009) alongside A-list stars Liam Neeson, Julianne Moore and Amanda Seyfried. Working with such big names left Nina gobsmacked: 'Amanda and I are friends now, but she's such an incredible actress, and she's someone I was star-struck about, too... I mean, c'mon, *Mean Girls*? *Mamma Mia*? She was unreal.'

But it wasn't enough for Nina, who was hungry for more: while the movies were good experience, they were still only supporting roles. Her biggest role and most high-profile part to date had been in an MTV-produced television movie called *American Mall* (2008), which was produced by the same people behind Disney's *High School Musical*. In this, Nina had to uncover a previously unknown talent for singing: 'It was

my first time going in the studio, and recording and doing that whole thing so I had help, I definitely had help. The whole experience was surreal.' It was a boost to her profile and helped Nina to prove to herself and her friends and family that she could make it. But really breaking out would require some big decision making and little did she know, once she made that decision a massive audition was waiting just around the corner…

Nina knew that if she wanted to seriously pursue acting, she would have to move to LA, so in 2009 she packed up her Toronto life and moved to the City of Angels to try her luck. And luck was definitely on her side: her first audition for her first pilot was for *The Vampire Diaries*. Unfortunately, though, on the day of the audition Nina just wasn't up to her best.

Kevin Williamson remembered seeing her the first time and – shockingly – he wasn't 100 per cent convinced: 'Nina came in for us one day to audition. She was sick, she had the flu – worst audition ever. We didn't even look at her a second time. And she went home, went back to Canada, and she was just miserable. She's like, "I was sick, I was just awful – I can do better than that." So she put herself on video tape and she sent that tape through, and we put it in and we were like, "Who's that?" "Oh, she came in and auditioned." "No, she didn't." "Oh, the sick girl?" She was a totally different girl, totally.' It seems Kevin has a lot of luck in finding leading ladies from video tapes, as that was exactly how he found Katie Holmes for *Dawson's Creek* – by watching her VHS audition.

Paul Wesley can relate to Nina's casting story – he's flubbed many an audition, too. 'Once, I finished a read, looked at the director and said, "That didn't go very well, did it?" He gave me a stern look, crossed his arms and said, "No, it didn't."' he told *VMan* magazine. 'I was devastated.'

Nina worked really hard putting together the audition tape, knowing that second chances were rare in Hollywood. Tons of girls were auditioning for the part and she knew that she'd have to put in the performance of a lifetime if she was to make a good impression, so in between filming scenes for the movie *Chloe*, Nina filmed herself for *The Vampire Diaries*: 'I put myself on a tape. It was the scene from the pilot where I'm in the graveyard alone and I'm talking to the crow. It was a really awkward audition to do!'

Kevin Williamson and Julie Plec loved the tape and none of the actresses they had seen could compare but there was still one nagging issue – in the original L.J. Smith books, the character of Elena has beautiful long, blonde hair. Nina, of course, was a brunette and with her stunning Bulgarian olive skin, she wouldn't be convincing if they dyed her hair a natural blonde. 'When we set out to cast Elena, we hoped to find a beautiful blonde actress,' Julie admits. 'That being said, we have to build a television series that can run for many years and it hinges around the actress who brings Elena to life.' For that, they decided upon Nina. 'And we're not sorry,' Julie is quick to add.

'Once we zeroed in on her [Nina], we were done. Done!' reiterated Kevin.

Still, even with Kevin and Julie's endorsement, Nina still had a number of people to convince: 'They liked [my tape], so I flew in and auditioned in front of the studio, then the network, then the producers. It was very nerve-wracking, especially when you're standing in front of so many influential and powerful people.'

As it happened, the network and the producers loved her, too: Nina had the part. What she didn't realise, however, was that she was actually going to be playing *two* characters on the

show. It was a huge moment for her, as she knew that she was really going to get the chance to show off her skills and versatility. She told SpoilerTV: 'When I first auditioned, I worked really hard and crossed my fingers that I would get the part of Elena. I had no idea I would also be playing Katherine. Much later Katherine was introduced into the script through the flashbacks and I found out I was both Elena and Katherine. It raised the stakes and changed the opportunity from just the role of a girl next door to two very conflicting and different challenges.'

She really relished the chance to do it and searched down deep to find enough real-life experience to play both roles convincingly. 'The two characters appeal to different parts of me and feed different parts of my soul,' she said (although of course she relates more closely to Elena!). 'I really admire the fact that Katherine looks out for herself. I think you need to have a selfish period in life, where you discover yourself. My work is so demanding and the hours are so long and the [material] so heavy. In the off-time I have, I'm sort of selfish. I stay home and I sleep a lot. I'm actually slowly becoming a vampire.' She was also lucky that she had co-star Ian Somerhalder to bounce off. The two seemed to feed off each other's energy and Nina actually stole a few of Ian's moves for Katherine! 'Damon gets a lot of who he is from Katherine, because he's basically learned everything that he knows about being a vampire from her so I actually adopted Ian's performance and some of Ian's quirks, so that the transition would make sense. Damon picked things up from Katherine, so in turn I drew inspiration from Ian. She enjoys being devious and I took a lot of that from Ian. Katherine and Damon are two of a kind,' Nina explained to *LA Times*.

She also had to learn how to flip very quickly between

characters and faced the difficult task of acting against herself (like Phoebe and her twin sister Ursula in *Friends* or Lindsay Lohan in the movie, *The Parent Trap*): 'I get to play against myself in a scene, which is both challenging and interesting at the same time. I really just have to stay focused on the moment and the motivation behind whichever character I shoot first and allow myself to transition when it's time to switch. I have to plan my actions and movements, and remember to react to them when we shoot the reverse/other character.'

Nina might have been tackling the challenges and feeling like she was slowly becoming a vampire, but she wasn't to be allowed to shun the spotlight for long. Her casting was one of the first big announcements made about *The Vampire Diaries* and she was subsequently catapulted into the limelight. When her ex-producers on *Degrassi* heard the news, they sent her a huge bouquet of flowers to congratulate her.

But the hard work had only just begun: now that Kevin and Julie had the perfect Elena, they really needed the right Stefan.

Chapter Eight

The Boy with the Fangs

Damon: It is what it is, Elena. The Stefan you know is good-behaviour Stefan, rein-it-in Stefan, fight-against-his-nature-to-an-annoyingly-obsessive-level Stefan. But if you think there's not another part to this, then you have not been paying attention.

Elena: He is not you, not even close.

Damon: Well, he doesn't want to be me. That doesn't mean deep down that he's not…

(1.18, 'Under Control')

'The very last role to be cast of our series was Stefan,' revealed Julie Plec, during a DVD extras video. But what was it about Stefan that was so hard to get right?

Stefan Salvatore is the pivotal role in the entire series: both the hero and the anti-hero, he is essentially a good person but only because he constantly restrains his darker side. Although he initially believed he was in love with Katherine, he soon realises that it was only her manipulations and glamouring that made him believe this. He is the reluctant vampire, who is so repulsed by his innate need to kill people that he suppresses the desire, making the choice to go 'vegetarian' and feed only on animals; Stefan is the vampire

with a moral conscience. It's only once he finds Elena that he discovers the meaning of true love and how hard it is for him to control himself when he's around her. Paul Wesley has a startlingly difficult physical brief to match, with the script calling for Stefan Salvatore to be a 'gloriously, amazingly, epically beautiful young man, elegant and ageless', who has to appear to be only seventeen years old, though in actuality he is 165.

Of equal importance was the chemistry between the two leads. 'The relationship between Elena and Stefan had to be magic,' said one producer on the show. Indeed, it turned out to be the most difficult casting challenge *The Vampire Diaries*' team had to face. Nina remembers screen testing with lots of guys and there were few standouts. The exception, of course, was Paul. 'He had this old-soul, historic feel about him,' she recalls.

For Paul, it was also excruciatingly painful. 'Oh my God, hardest I've ever worked for a part! I auditioned for the role of Damon three times, four times maybe. Constantly went back for Damon, back and forth, back and forth. They wouldn't see me for Stefan, they thought I wasn't right for it.'

It was his handsome good looks that made the studio think Damon as opposed to Stefan, at least initially: 'I think physically they thought I represented Damon more. I think they were envisioning someone even more innocent for Stefan.'

Eventually, of course, they decided on the sexy Ian Somerhalder for the role of Damon. As they had ended up with a much older Damon than originally intended, they went back to Paul, thinking, 'Maybe this will work': 'They brought me in for Stefan and I read for it, like four times.' In fact, even though originally, they would only see him for Damon, it was always Stefan who Paul himself felt drawn to: 'I had in my mind that

Stefan was the character I wanted to play,' he recalls. '[He] felt more inherent to my own personality. I am a diehard, hopeless romantic. He's melancholic and I have that dark side that gets very melancholic.'

Melancholy aside, the competition to play Stefan was fierce. With the success of the male leads in *Twilight* and *True Blood*, it was clear to everyone that scoring a part as a vampire (even a minor one, let alone a leading role!) was a quick route to superstardom. Hence actors flew in from all over the world to compete for the role. Paul remembers screen testing against 'three guys from Australia, three guys from London, four guys from New York, five guys from LA. It was like *American Idol*. It was like "go home… go home…" and "you stay… you stay…"' One of those guys testing for Stefan against Paul was *Friday Night Lights*' actor Grey Damon but although he wasn't chosen for this vampiric role, he did find himself on *True Blood* (as Kitch Maynard) a year or so later.

It was early March 2009 and getting close to crunch time. Every other major role was filled and the pilot was ready to start shooting in Vancouver. Kevin Williamson and Julie Plec just couldn't seem to be able to make up their minds about Stefan and so, unlike every other role in the series, they sent the tapes up to the producers without a specific person in mind or a recommendation.

Peter Roth, one of the producers, saw Paul Wesley in the role and immediately told Kevin and Julie: 'That's your guy.' Their reaction was: 'Really?'

To say they weren't entirely convinced is an understatement, but under the time constraints they hired Paul for the pilot anyway. He was thrilled, even though he knew he had a lot to prove – and not just to the producers: 'I wanted to prove to

myself that I had the versatility to take on such a role. Stefan is just so complex, there's so much going on. When I read the script, I just loved it. I got so excited. I can't explain it, but there was something about Stefan that just invigorated me,' he told Zap2It.com.

It wasn't until five days into the shoot when Paul did his first-ever scene (it's the one with Elena running through the fog-filled cemetery) that the producers had a sudden realisation: there was real chemistry between Paul and Nina. 'It was phenomenal... Kevin and I just...' [Julie gasps here]. 'He is our guy. I can only apologise to the whole world for taking so long to realise how good Paul Wesley was,' she said.

'We chose Paul because he has so much range,' Kevin told *SFX*. 'Right now we're playing him as serious Stefan, straight guy to his brother who gets the fun stuff, but the interesting thing about Stefan is I think he has the better journey. Damon is a bad guy through and through. He may try to be good every now and again, but he's never going to be too good. Stefan, however, has been going against the grain for the last hundred years. He hasn't had human blood, which makes it an internalised struggle and there will come a time when he will drink blood. When that happens, the shit's going to hit the fan!'

Paul's hard work had paid off; he was rewarded with a great part and it seemed like everything he had done in his life prior to *The Vampire Diaries* had been leading up to that very moment: 'I don't know how I got [the part] but I will have to say, I've been on my own since I was sixteen years old and that's a long time. I think if they went with the guy who just left his parents' house I don't know if he could pull off being 160 years old. I guess I got lucky. I think you have to

have this innate sort of energy that is sort of 160 years old, where people look at you in the eye and they go, "You've experienced something."'

He took inspiration from his grandfather on how to play 160 years of wisdom and was humble enough to admit that at first he didn't feel wise enough: 'I was a little nervous, because it's a lot to think about. I have to encompass 160 years of knowledge in my brain and I'm twenty-seven, and I'm thinking about the wisdom of my grandfather who is eighty, who is my hero. And I'm thinking about how wise he is and I'm twice his age.'

Of course, maybe it helped that Paul seemed destined to play a vampire – after all, he comes with his very own set of fangs! He once joked at an Armani after-party that he almost blew his audition for the hit CW show, until he showed off his secret weapon: his natural vampire fangs. But Kevin and Julie hadn't noticed his pointed canines until after the casting, so he really can't attribute his success to them! It did make Nina wonder, though. 'I am still unsure about whether Paul is or isn't a vampire,' she told *Nylon* magazine. 'Obviously there's the teeth, but also he just kept showing up everywhere. I would be out with the girls, having lunch or going shopping, and he would just be there, out of nowhere.' That makes him a vampire in her eyes!

Paul was extremely excited to get to work with Kevin Williamson: 'I grew up with *Dawson's Creek* and I always watched it. In fact, since then I have a deep admiration for Kevin Williamson, both for this show and for *Scream*: it is still strange to think that a figure who influenced so much my childhood now has chosen me to work with him!'

He was intimidated, however, by the constant comparisons between himself and Robert Pattinson. 'I basically get it

every day, in every interview I do,' said Paul. It was the natural comparison to make – Robert's Edward was very similar to Paul's Stefan, in that they were both high-school age, vampire-vegetarians and in love with a human girl. 'I think nine out of ten girls would throw me under a bus to get to Edward Cullen,' observed Paul, with typical modesty. 'In all sincerity I just want to create a character that is independent of that.'

He wasn't really aware of the whole *Twilight* thing and he definitely hadn't watched the movies yet he decided that he owed it to himself – and to the genre – to have a little look at what all the fuss was about. 'Prior to shooting the pilot, I had never seen *Twilight*,' he admitted during a *The Vampire Diaries*' press tour. 'I specifically went out of my way to not watch *Twilight* because I didn't want it to in any way influence me because I knew that it was a similar subject matter. And now, I've actually never watched the movie in its entirety, but I've seen parts of it. I was impressed because it has this – not to make this about *Twilight*, but it has this super sort of youthful following. And I found it pretty engaging, so I was kind of relatively surprised. You know what I mean? I didn't think – I thought it would be a lot campier. I actually liked it, what I saw.' It goes to show that just as the cast didn't want people to judge *The Vampire Diaries* before they had seen it, Paul shouldn't have judged *Twilight* either!

Now twenty-seven years old, Paul had been at this point before: a great cast, lots of buzz, a pilot script that was well written and executed; he really wanted to throw everything into his role in order to make it a success. He knew that he wouldn't truly be able to understand Stefan unless he got to know the character and so he headed straight for his nearest book store,

bought the books and devoured the series: 'The minute I was cast, I ploughed through all the books.'

At least he was prepared for how much Kevin and Julie were about to change…

Chapter Nine

Getting into Character

Stefan: I know that it's hard to understand but I'm doing this for you.

Elena: No, you don't get to make that decision for me. If you walk away, it's for you, because I know what I want. Stefan, I love you.

(1.10, 'The Turning Point')

With the show veering off into a completely different direction from the books, Paul didn't gain too much plot-wise from reading them. However, by reading all about the 'original' Stefan, he proved that he really was trying to delve as deep into his character as possible. It's evidence once more of Paul's dedication to his craft and his love of method acting. He likes to get right down into the role and uncover the hidden meanings behind why his character might act the way he does.

Getting so involved has its drawbacks, though: Paul hardly has any time for anything else. 'I don't have a personal life,' he told *Post Gazette*. 'I'm not complaining, but I literally don't have a personal life. Let me put it this way: When I wasn't on this show

and I had a lot of personal life, I was much more miserable so let's just leave it at that.'

He wasn't about to complain too much because this was the role he had been waiting for his whole life – the kind of part he could really sink his teeth into (pun fully intended). With the success of the pilot and subsequent episodes, it was clear that this show had a long shelf-life. For once, all the work and development that Paul wanted to put into his character was going to pay off.

After years of playing mythological creatures, from werewolves to angels, Paul was ready to play a vampire. He still wasn't a massive fantasy fan per se (although he needs to drop that attitude and just accept that he is destined for a life of fantasy!), but the idea of vampires really appealed to him: 'What's great about a vampire is you can incorporate it into real world circumstances, rather than *Lord of the Rings*, where you're in *Lord of the Rings*' world,' he told *Women's Wear Daily*. 'This is this mysterious, dark, dangerous, omniscient being in the world. The character is very much like the rebellious, sexual, iconic figure that throughout the years we've always felt this need to get to know. Like the Marlon Brando.'

Some of the easiest scenes for Paul to play are when Stefan gets angry (and let's face it, that's mostly after the taunts of his brother, Damon, or when someone threatens his beloved Elena!). For angry Stefan, Paul channels his younger, rebellious self – the Paul who would start fights in school and slam people into boards on the ice-hockey rink: 'I just imagine all the blood rushing to my face, all the temptation and anger. I actually have anger. I'm not saying I'm like a violent person but I have an anger that is inherent, that I've always had. So when I'm doing scenes with Ian and he's driving me crazy on screen, it's kind of easy for me to tap into it and I just let the

anger out in that way.' He also gets to channel his more serious and sensitive side as Stefan, although unlike his character, he's never quite kept a diary. 'I don't [do it] religiously, but writing has always been very therapeutic for me,' he told *Pop Wrap*. 'But if you think about it, Stefan was turned into a vampire during the Civil War, so he's been around for roughly 150 years, so how do you remember all that info? You have to keep a journal of some kind, so he has this massive cabinet where he keeps all those journals.'

In fact, his favourite episode to shoot throughout the entire first season was called 'The Turning Point': 'It was a really beautiful episode for Stefan and Elena. The moment where he turns around because he's ashamed of his face – the blood is rushing through his eyes, his veins are popping out – he's terrified, and he hates himself for it. He runs from that part of himself, but she turns him around and tells him not to be afraid. She touches his face and she thinks he's beautiful. It's so intimate, that moment, because she accepts the darkest part of him.'

That particular scene is very indicative of Stefan throughout most of the first season of *The Vampire Diaries*. He is very straight-laced; he's brooding, he's steadfast in his love for Elena, he doesn't drink blood from humans and he wants almost more than anything to rebuild a good relationship with his brother but throughout the series, Stefan evolves into a much more complex person as his character is faced with challenges that will make or break him when it comes to his morals. Paul enjoys getting to play this shift in personality: 'I love it. I love not necessarily the dark side – I mean, I love that as well – I like Stefan to have some other tactics other than being victimised and accepting. And I want him to be more proactive.'

Paul found that one good way of imagining how Stefan would feel is to think of him as a recovering drug addict: he could slip and fall into temptation at any time – after all, he is constantly surrounded by his 'drug' – human blood – and it is only his personal code of ethics that keeps him in check. 'No wonder Damon is so damn chipper,' said Paul, comparing his character to Ian's. 'He's like a junkie with heroin growing in his backyard, with clean needles everywhere! It's perfect! Damon is always high; he's having a blast! The moment Stefan lets go of his guilt and consumes that human blood and indulges, he's going to be high and it's going to be like a split personality.' A character with a split personality? It's every method actor's dream come true! Paul gets to bring variety to the role to prevent him from ever becoming bored.

Another way that he gets into character is through Stefan's style. Jennifer Bryan, costume designer on the show, told *Entertainment Weekly* about how she chose Stefan's style, as opposed to Damon's: 'Damon's style is very narrow. With Stefan, I can do a little bit more because he's in high school. I do a little bit more colour on him because at one point, we felt that we needed to separate them so they didn't start to look alike.' Hand-in-glove with style, was Paul's own physical appearance. He felt as if he had to embody the vampire in every way, which meant altering his physique somewhat: 'I feel like vampires are these svelte creatures whose nutrition is essentially animal blood, so I knew that I couldn't eat all these different carbs and sugars because it just didn't feel right, physically and mentally so I've been limiting my intake, just because I feel like that's what Stefan does, every day. For the first time in my life, I've been doing cardio,' he told *IESB*. Now that's dedication! It also appeared to be working, as in 2010 Paul was named one of *People* magazine's Sexiest Men Alive.

As for the real benefits of being a vampire, getting bored is the main drawback of eternal life as far as Paul is concerned: 'With the ageless thing you'd be bored as hell, everyone you know would die. I think everyone wants eternal life and everyone is scared of death but come on, if you think about it, it would be pretty miserable. The ambiguity and mystery of life is gone, you know what you're going to be doing until the sun explodes! Death is a part of life and when I first got the part I thought to myself, "What is Stefan so tormented about?" But then when I put myself in his mind frame I thought, "You know what? It would be pretty miserable to never get old."'

Although it seems like Paul should know a little bit about never aging, considering he's played a teenager almost his entire life (even now, at the tender age of twenty-seven). Even when he starred as a high-school student in *Fallen* when he was just twenty-four years old, he was asked the question about whether he would prefer more 'adult' roles. It turns out, he just wasn't considered suitable by most casting directors: 'Yeah, you just sort of get over it. I've been doing it for so many years. I met with some people last week to play a young lawyer and they are like, "We love him but he can't play a lawyer" [too young-looking]. So, I'm looking forward to some day playing some more mature characters.'

That day doesn't seem close at hand, not with a character eternally stuck in his teenage body! Meanwhile, Paul's not sure what he'll do if the show continues to be a success: 'Honestly, I'd have to use a lot of sleep and moisturiser,' he joked. But he's not the only adult playing the part of a teenager, not even close. Other hit television shows such as *90210* and *Glee* are filled with adult actors playing teen roles. In *90210*, Trevor Donovan is thirty-one years old and playing high-schooler Teddy Montgomery – that's older than Ryan Eggold, who plays his

teacher and is only twenty-five! *Glee* is another culprit, as high-school jocks Finn Hudson and Puck Puckerman are both played by twenty-seven-year-olds: Cory Monteith and Mark Salling, respectively. No one really seems to mind, though – it's the acting that counts! – although Paul might struggle to play a convincing seventeen-year-old as the seasons go on.

Playing such an intense character did take its toll on Paul, however: 'Season One was incredibly taxing on me because I got a little too almost method and it got a little bit intense for me as far as affecting my personal being,' he told *Women's Wear Daily*. 'I've made a very conscientious decision to try not to take home what I do at work, which I was not really capable of at first but I realised this is a marathon, not a sprint, so I'm preparing myself for the long run.'

For the first time since he started performing, *The Vampire Diaries* had given Paul that double-edged sword of acting: fame. Of course he wanted to be famous – to keep on being offered big, juicy parts, to build his profile and his résumé and his career, he *had* to be famous but becoming a teen icon is fame on a different level – as the actors in *Twilight* had already experienced tenfold. Funnily enough, that's something else Paul shares with Robert Pattinson: a slightly reclusive edge to his personality that makes him sometimes resent the lack of privacy given him in his new role as superstar.

For Paul, this meant that many of life's simple pleasures were removed. Things he took for granted, such as exploring his favourite city, New York, were now no longer possible: 'I'm a city boy, and I thrive off of culture. Something about being on the streets of Manhattan revives me, so walking around and not having anonymity and just being recognised would really take away that experience of being in a city.'

Perhaps one of the stranger sides of fame could only occur

because he became famous for playing a vampire: 'I was at a bar in Atlanta and this one girl asked me to bite her,' he revealed to George Lopez on his late-night show. 'I think I was a little drunk and I was like, yeah, I'm gonna do it this time! I'm just gonna see where this goes. I think she was expecting a really sexy bite, like on the neck, and I just felt uncomfortable so I sort of really reluctantly grabbed her arm, and I kind of like, just drooled on it a little bit. I like, bit it and I think I hurt her and she was oddly repulsed.' So remember, if you're a fan of Paul's and you get to meet him one day, don't ask him to bite you!

Indeed Paul's fascinated by the fans who *aren't* the norm. Everyone thinks of *The Vampire Diaries* as solely teen territory, but some of his fan encounters would indicate that that's just not the case! 'It's very quickly become apparent that a lot of people watch the show. When I do go places now, I find the oddest people coming up to me. The businessman in the elevator, who's just standing there minding his own business in awkward silence, goes, "Love your show." That kind of thing happens all the time. It's awesome!'

Another, sweeter benefit of being famous has come from his two biggest fans – his younger sisters. 'They have read all of *The Vampire Diaries*' books – they are my only fans, actually. Them and my mom,' he laughs. He's been able to help out with his siblings' popularity, too – just by picking them up from school or attending their birthday parties, much to the delight of all their friends!

Chapter Ten

The Other Boys

Damon: A room full of women clamouring to go out on a date with me? Sounds tasty. (1.15, 'A Few Good Men')

It wasn't only Paul Wesley and Ian Somerhalder who received a huge profile lift from their experience in *The Vampire Diaries*. The same went for the rest of the gorgeous men in the supporting cast roles – Steven R. McQueen, Zach Roerig, Michael Trevino and Joseph Morgan, who was cast as Klaus in January 2011.

Steven R. McQueen, born Steven Chadwick McQueen (the 'R' in his initials stand for Robitaille, which is his step-dad's surname) on 13 July 1988 in Los Angeles, California, was one of the first to be announced as part of *The Vampire Diaries*' cast, alongside Nina Dobrev. He was hardly a stranger to fame – his grandfather was the 'King of Cool' actor Steve McQueen, who made his name in *The Magnificent Seven* (1960), *The Great Escape* (1963), and *The Thomas Crown Affair* (1968). Yet even

with that impressive family lineage, he didn't try to get into acting straightaway. He didn't really have the chance to – he was constantly moving around with his mum and stepdad, Luc Robitaille, a professional hockey player who won the Stanley Cup with the Detroit Red Wings but also played for the Pittsburgh Penguins, New York Rangers and the Los Angeles Kings. Steven was home-schooled, so he never really got the chance to set up a base and develop real friendships – or even attend his own prom! And so he turned to movies – including those starring his famous grandfather, who died before Steven was born. 'I watched my grandfather's projects with admiration and looked up to him, but at the end of the day you have to be true to what's inside,' he told *Vanity Fair*.

After Steven moved back to Los Angeles at the age of seventeen, he was bitten by the acting bug and once he started, he just couldn't stop: 'Once I started doing it I knew it was something I would love. It just kind of became my passion. I've been blessed and pretty much worked ever since,' he told *MTV*.

And he was luckier than most – one of his first jobs was a recurring role on the American TV drama series *Everwood* (2002–06), in which he played Kyle Hunter, a young bad boy musical prodigy, whose experience of 'coming out' on the show was considered an inspiration to a lot of gay teens. It was a steep learning curve for Steven, who didn't have much experience at that time. He was learning from the best, however: 'I've learned more and more on each show that I've done. I've been blessed and I've gotten to work with some very talented actors – James Gandolfini, Treat Williams... I've kind of always asked for advice and tried to take in as much as I could, whenever working with them.' He worked with James Gandolfini on a short movie called *Club Soda* (2006) and landed the leading role in *Minutemen* (2008) a Disney Channel movie.

Steven hopped around the television circuit, adding shows such as *Numb3rs*, *CSI: Miami* and *Without a Trace* to his résumé then suddenly he was in demand for *two* new hit shows on The CW: *Melrose Place* and *The Vampire Diaries*. At that point, it was impossible to determine which show was to be the more successful. *Melrose Place* had a big name attached to it – Ashlee Simpson-Wentz, who we have already met in the earlier chapter about Nina Dobrev – and the original 1990s' series *Melrose Place* was an enormous success. Still, it was the character of Jeremy that really appealed to him. 'I was auditioning for [*The Vampire Diaries*] and *Melrose Place*, and I was getting up to the testing for [*The Vampire Diaries*]. I enjoyed the script and I liked the idea of vampires as people who don't follow the rules of humanity. My character was this self-destructive kid who's lost his parents and is rebelling against the world. I got really excited about that, and auditioned for it and landed it,' he told IESB.com.

Jeremy Gilbert was a character created specifically for the show as he didn't feature in the original *Vampire Diaries*' books. In the books, Elena actually has a younger sister named Margaret Gilbert, rather than a brother, and she was much younger – only four years old, as opposed to Jeremy's fifteen. 'The book fans were a little testy about that because Margaret played an integral part in one plot point that they liked quite a bit,' Julie Plec told *Soap Opera Weekly*. 'But I was sitting there with (co-executive producer/writer) Kevin Williamson trying to think, "How are we going to write a story for a four-year-old, cast a good four-year-old, and give them anything to do other than sit there and look cute?" You're biting off a lot more than you want to.' And so it was that Jeremy was created to bring additional conflict into Elena's life.

Steven, for one, is glad that they made the change! In a video

interview for The CW, he said: 'When our characters are closer in age, it allows us to interact in more ways than we would be able to if I was a young girl. But sorry, fans, that I'm not Margaret [laughs]... and in pre-school. Well, mentally I might be, but...'

The new character Jeremy is highly tormented and in the first few episodes he is seen taking and dealing drugs – the part of the show that L.J. Smith had the most issues with – but for Steven, Jeremy's torment was his appeal: 'My character, he's not a vampire, but he's got all the attributes: he's pale, he looks like he hasn't slept in a while so he becomes the guilty-seeming figure when he's mad. But a lot of vampires are naturally beautiful and look very together and are trying to get away with everything: I'm the rebel without a cause.'

In the meantime, he also made his most high-profile movie appearance to date, as main character Jake Forester in the 3D comedy-horror romp *Piranha 3D* (2010). The movie was about a school of evil-looking prehistoric piranhas who are unleashed into a lake to devour unsuspecting college students on their spring break. Almost 1,000 characters were killed off in the film: 'I think we used more blood than any movie ever has,' Steven admitted to Filmcritic.com. 'We actually had an oil tanker standing by, so fake blood could just be pumping out all day. It's so funny, man. I went from Disney, which caters to a youthful audience, to *The Vampire Diaries* and now *Piranha*. It's fun to see the different ways I can entertain different audiences.'

It definitely seems like the ability to entertain runs through his blood. He doesn't just want to sit in his grandfather's shadow, however, and he told *Vanity Fair*, 'Luckily, I've got a generation gap between me and him but more than anything, it's a little fuel in the fire.' Also, he doesn't believe that having a famous last name has given him any advantage over the competition – or rather,

any advantage he might have gleaned is taken away by the added expectation: 'Well, it leans both ways. People are excited to meet with me and that helps, but then when you get into the meeting or audition, they expect you to be great so it adds a little bit of pressure but it makes things more interesting,' he told *People* magazine. Sometimes he has to put up with a little ribbing about his grandfather, however, and he was once pulled over by the police, 'and the officer thought my ID was fake,' he laughed to *Teen Vogue*.

Someone who's had to forge his own path to success in Hollywood, without any famous relatives as an extra boost, is Zachary George 'Zach' Roerig, who plays Elena's childhood best friend and ex-boyfriend Matt Donovan. Zach's birthday is on 22 February 1985. He grew up in Montpelier, Ohio, a small town where he had a relatively normal childhood playing on his high-school wrestling and American football teams.

Zach spent his summers working in his family's business, Fackler Monuments, where he had the morbid task of helping to make gravestones. 'I'd been doing that since I was able to tie my own work boots. I'm from a really, really small town in Ohio and it was always set up that I was going to be the guy to take over the business,' he told *Teen Vogue*. But it seems destiny had another path for Zach and while in high school, he decided that he wanted to act – or at least, give it a try – before he settled down forever as a stonemason. He heard an announcement on the radio that an agency in Cleveland was scouting for young people who were looking to get into acting or modelling and so he decided to give it a shot and see whether he had any talent for acting at all: 'When I was like, sixteen I drove to Cleveland every weekend to study at a small boutique acting school – it's actually the same school that Sean Faris started out at, and that's how I knew him before he

came on the show [as Mystic Grill's bartender Ben McKittrick].' The boutique acting school was Stone Model and Talent, Barbizon of Cleveland, which is pretty funny when you consider that Zach might have been going into a totally different type of stonework!

With his all-American good looks, athletic body and deep blue eyes, Zach wasn't only popular in high school (although he definitely *was* popular – he was his high-school's prom king!), he was completely in demand as a model. After finishing high school, he took off for bigger and better things in New York City. He dropped Stone Model agency for the massive Ford Models and straightaway started booking jobs. In 2003, he was even named Most Sought After Male at the huge modelling showcase run by the International Modeling and Talent Association. He did some basic catalogue work and filmed a commercial for St. John's University, in which he played a college student. Then, finally, a proper acting gig: he was cast as Casey Hughes on the soap opera, *As the World Turns.* His first episode aired 18 January 2005 and he stayed on the series for two years (until 2 May 2007), turning down other acting gigs in order to remain on the show.

After his stint on *As the World Turns* was over, he jumped ship to another soap opera, *One Life to Live*. A few movies fell his way too (including *Assassination of a High School President* [2008], in which he played another character of Irish descent named Matt), but he was especially psyched when he landed a role that enabled him to share his love of the great outdoors. He was cast as a cowboy in the drama *Friday Night Lights*, a series based around a high-school football team: 'I'm a country boy from Ohio. I rode horses since I was a kid. When I booked the job they asked if I could ride. I got to go out there about two weeks before we started filming. I trained with cowboys on a ranch. It was really cool.'

Yet, none of Zach's roles so far had been particularly life changing but little did he know that someone was keeping a close eye on his career. That person was Kevin Williamson. Kevin had seen an acting audition that Zach had taped and he knew that he wanted to work with him. He kept track on his appearances on *As the World Turns* but the right role proved elusive. Zach continued to attend auditions for Kevin's shows and yet walked away empty-handed. 'Zach is a guy I've had my eye on for a while,' Kevin told the *LA Times*. 'I actually brought him in to the network for the lead in *Hidden Palms* (2007) and that role ultimately went to Taylor [Handley]. Zach wasn't right for that role, but when the character of Matt came up I thought of him right away.'

When he finally scored the part of Matt Donovan on *The Vampire Diaries*, Zach was over the moon: 'I am honoured to work with Kevin Williamson because I've been trying to work with him for years. I tried out for a few pilots in the past that he had written and the network thought other people were right and chose them but Kevin kept bringing me in for stuff and we were finally able to work together.'

Despite vampires being all the rage, Zach was actually happy not to be playing one. 'When it first started out I was totally content not playing a vampire just because there's a lot of extra contacts and make-up involved,' he told Fancast. But all that changed once he saw just how much fun the vamps were having! 'Ian Somerhalder makes it look like a blast,' he admitted ruefully. Don't worry, Zach: there's always a chance that Kevin and Julie will turn you into a vampire! However, that might not be a great thing for Zach-fans, as apart from the key three vamps (Stefan, Damon and Katherine), most don't seem to last very long before they get a stake through the heart!

The part of Matt seemed custom-designed for Zach: 'I

would like to think that I am quite similar to Matt in terms of his protectiveness as well as his general good-heartedness; although I don't think I have near the temperament that he shows at times.' Zach is very protective of his younger sister, Emily, although she's not so much of a troublemaker as Vicki is! In the show Matt is a football player, which suits Zach just fine: 'I'm a huge fan of the football stuff because I played in high school.' He is also one of the characters least-changed from the original book persona. Julie Plec told *Soap Opera Weekly*, 'on most shows you don't get that hot, well-liked athlete, who also happens to be a good person and have a good heart.' Zach agrees, although he thinks that Matt might one day be driven to the edge: 'Two reasons I don't think Matt should be messed with,' he told *Starry Constellation Mag*. 'First, because TV needs a nice guy like Matt, a guy that is pure and doesn't have a motive at the end of the day. Second, you never, ever want to mess with the most polite, quiet athlete type because you know they're always hiding some kind of secret and by the time you try to mess with them, all hell will break loose. I think Matt's got some hidden rage – I mean, look at his life, he's never exhibited any ounce of anger or emotion and so I feel like it's going to be a Ned Flanders' kind of explosion.'

Unlike his character, who has a tense relationship with his sister and is more of a parent to his wild-child mother than she ever was to him, Zach is extremely close to his family. His real mother, Andrea, is extremely proud of him and 100 per cent supportive. She told *Toledo Blade*: 'He was always very good about coming home. He is just a really good, generous, big-hearted person. I hope that part of him never changes.'

His big-hearted nature doesn't look like it's going to go anywhere anytime soon. Zach is about more than acting now: he is on the board of a company called Glass Ceiling Media,

whose goal is to break down barriers in the media world, with a mission statement to: 'understand, enhance, and monetize social media'. Zach explained on a podcast via *Portrait Magazine* why they chose the name: 'Glass ceiling is usually a term that represents limitations and we chose the name because using digital and social media to produce provocative content we are going to defy limitation.' With a company like that, you can expect that Zach is a pro on all the social networking sites (switch over to the Damon side to find out more about *The Vampire Diaries* on Twitter and to see how to get in touch with him there).

One thing is for sure, Zach is infinitely grateful to *The Vampire Diaries* for giving him so many opportunities: 'When I started this, it was so I could be able to do all the other things I wanted to do, like build a barn. The dream was always to do feature films, but this is the best job. Every single one of us on this show now has a dollar sign above our head. Our foreign value is going through the roof. We're huge all over the world.'

Another non-vampire hottie is Michael Trevino, who plays bad-boy-with-a-secret Tyler Lockwood. He's a California native with Mexican heritage, 'I'm a full-blooded Mexican,' he told Latina.com. 'My mother was born in Zacatecas, Mexico, and my father – the son of Mexican immigrants – was born near Fresno, California.' Unlike Paul Wesley and Nina Dobrev, that doesn't mean he speaks his parents' native language, though and it's probably Michael's biggest regret. 'I was brought up bilingual, but there came a point where my mom went back to work and I got a white babysitter, so sadly I lost it. Now I can understand Spanish and put words together, but I don't speak it fluently – I'm ashamed of that.'

Michael was born on 25 January 1985. Coming from California meant that the transition into acting wasn't a difficult

one, especially not for someone as gorgeous as Michael! Yet despite his good looks and although, like Zach, he was a jock in high school and on the football team, he wasn't nearly as popular. 'It was weird, like I was the jock, I played football all four years of high school, but for some reason I always got picked on. I don't know what it was man, maybe I was yapping my mouth too much or maybe people were threatened, I don't know what it is.' Needless to say, he was keen to get out of there and start the rest of his life.

At first, he didn't really think of acting as a serious career. He did a commercial for the clothing company Old Navy, which gave him his first opening into the acting world but this exposure was limited as the commercial was only shown in one specific market: 'I booked that first, but it was only for the Spanish market so no one ever saw it... mainly all my friends, no one ever saw it 'cause I never told them.'

He went to college, but his acting dream just wouldn't die. While other young wannabe actors go to stage school or audition for an agency, Michael had a rather different approach: he went to his local bookstore and picked up a copy of *How To Be a Working Actor* by Mari Lyn Henry (a talent manager and former casting director) and Lynne Rogers (an actress). He studied hard and in the end, all of his hard work paid off. Meanwhile, he remained rather philosophical about it all: 'You gotta try, 'cause if not, it's always gonna linger in the back of your head.'

His first major role was as Jackson Meade in a Disney movie called *Cow Belles* (2006), which was the movie debut of teen pop singers Aly & AJ (Alyson and Amanda Michalka). The story follows two spoilt rich girls (played by Aly & AJ) as they are sent by their father to work on a dairy farm to teach them some life lessons. After short stops on *Commander in Chief* and

CSI: Miami, his first 'series regular' billing came with a television series called *Cane*, which aired in 2007. *Cane* was about a Cuban family who start up a rum and sugar-cane business. The series got great ratings when it opened, but due to the 2007–08 Writers Guild of America strike, which put many shows on hold, it was eventually cancelled. Michael was gutted: 'I was bummed when the show got cancelled. It was my first time as a series regular. I wanted it to keep going, because I was working with quality actors and having so much fun. I learned a lot from them.'

None of these roles had really given him any exposure to a wide audience, but that was about to change when he was cast as a love interest for AnnaLynne McCord's bitchy teen queen Naomi Clark on *90210*. He only appeared in four episodes but suddenly he was thrust into the limelight as a teen heartthrob. Following this, practically overnight his life changed. 'When I did *Cane*, [women] didn't recognise me. Once *90210* hit, it was weird! I was in Hollywood walking down the sidewalk with a couple of my buddies and these girls on the sidewalk were waiting to cross the street with us. One girl said, "Can I take a picture with you?" That doesn't necessarily happen a lot to me, to be honest.' At first he didn't really get along with his supposed love interest, although the feisty actress eventually won him over! 'I thought [AnnaLynne] was out of her mind because she's really out there and has so much energy but then we clicked big time,' he continued to Latina.com. It was a case of the two being *too* similar – as Michael shared that boundless energy and killer-watt star power. If he had a crush on anyone on set, though, it was for Jessica Lowndes, who plays Adrianna Tate-Duncan on the show.

After *90210*, the only way was up and when Michael heard about *The Vampire Diaries*, he knew this was his chance to fly

even higher. But it almost looked as if it wasn't going to happen: he told audiences at a convention in Australia that he auditioned and was turned down for the parts of Damon *and* Stefan before he finally got the call for Tyler. Michael went after the part with gusto: even though he wasn't going to play a vampire, he could be playing an even more interesting supernatural creature: a werewolf. 'I got the books and I was starting to do my research and I found out, oh, so he's a werewolf,' he told E! Online. 'I went into the audition knowing that. Kevin [Williamson] and Julie [Plec] said that would happen eventually on the show.' But don't worry: he didn't have to howl in his audition!

Tyler doesn't get much character development in the first season beyond being the 'human' bad boy who messes with Matt Donovan's sister, Vicki. Michael was frustrated because he truly believed that his character meant well: 'It was really easy to dislike Tyler but now we've seen the family that he comes from and what he has to deal with at home. He's not just this bully or punk; he has a heart. Yes, he has problems. Yes, he has a temper, but there's more humanity in him.' But he wasn't too frustrated about the lack of character movement because he knew he was in it for the long haul: 'You have to be patient, but then you understand that we have huge ensemble cast, we have to tell a story. There's a lot that's gonna happen in Season Two, there's a lot of surprises coming up, there's gonna be a lot more Tyler Lockwood coming around,' he promises.

He had to get in extra-good shape for the second season, too – even though he promises that *The Vampire Diaries*' werewolves will be different to the six-pack flaunting Taylor Lautner *Twilight* set: 'With all due respect to Taylor Lautner and his 18-pack abs, my werewolf is going to be 100 times cooler! This is going to be a whole different kind of werewolf. And right now,

there's a ton of werewolf stuff going on – series that are in development and werewolf spinoffs; I've got a lot to go up against. Just like Paul Wesley was compared to Rob Pattinson and vampires, I think I'm going to be thrown into the mix as far as werewolves go – so I'm kind of excited for that, because everybody's got their different take on the vampire genre and werewolf genre.'

In the show, Michael might be the typical bad boy who doesn't treat his girlfriends very well, but in real life he is much more romantic. He has recently been linked with *Glee* star Jenna Ushkowitz (Tina Cohen-Chang) and seems totally smitten.

The entire cast so far had been chosen well before the show took off, at a point when it was still uncertain whether the series would be a success but that wasn't the case for the role of Klaus. When Kevin Williamson and Julie Plec announced they were searching for a hot, young male actor to play the role of one of the oldest (and consequently, strongest) vampires in *The Vampire Diaries*' world, this was an opportunity that few could pass up. Klaus is one of the Originals, the first family of vampires, and he is the main antagonist in Season Two. He's out to hunt down Katherine and to break the curse that destroys vampires if they venture out into the sunlight but he doesn't actually appear onscreen until the very end of Season Two – which gave Kevin and Julie plenty of time to find the perfect actor and also provided lots of opportunity for the buzz and speculation to build.

A casting call showed up on vampire-diaries.net, one of the best and most dedicated of *The Vampire Diaries*' fan sites. It read: 'Klaus is late-20's (sic) to mid-30's (sic). He's handsome, charming, intelligent, with a sharp wit. He's the only person who can out-Damon, Damon. That's because he's got a thousand years on him. Klaus is one of the Originals. Possibly

the oldest. But you'd never know it because he keeps up with the times.' A vampire who can out-Damon, Damon? Ian Somerhalder had already established Damon as one of the most fun and charismatic characters on television, so Klaus would be a dream come true for whoever was lucky enough to nail the audition.

In a way, the character of Klaus was a treat for the book fans. Julie and Kevin had floated the idea of not using him at all but replacing him with another strong vampire called Phillippe, not related in any way to the book. But then they dropped the K-bomb (and this time, we're not talking 'Katherine'): 'We're gonna learn a lot about [Klaus] and be hopefully very afraid of him before we ever lay eyes on him,' Julie told *Entertainment Weekly*. 'That's gonna be a nice, big, long healthy tease. It's so funny, the way we dropped the bomb of his name last episode [Rose said The Originals, the oldest vampires, will be coming for Elena, and they'll be doing it for him, Klaus], Kevin and I were laughing. We're like, the book fans are gonna lose their freakin' minds in this moment, and the rest of America is gonna go, "Huh... Alright. Who's that?" [Laughs] But it's one of those moments that you're like, I don't care because I know the million book fans are gonna be so excited that it's worth it.'

Lots of actors' names were tossed into the ring by speculating fans and journalists alike. Everyone from older-guy hotties such as Ryan Phillippe (*Cruel Intentions*) and Milo Ventimiglia (*Heroes*) to former The CW stars like Joshua Jackson (*Dawson's Creek*) and Hal Ozsan, even actors who were *already* vampires such as Aleksander Skarsgard from *True Blood*. Kevin even joked that they had thought about just dyeing Ian's hair blond if they couldn't find anyone else!

Kevin and Julie were going to be picky and together, they watched over 200 auditions. 'I want that really great actor,'

Kevin told *Digital Spy*. 'We're looking at people that might be familiar to an audience, but more importantly we want the right role so I'm guessing it'll probably be someone we don't know.' Julie also thought it would be best not to cast an already famous face but to build someone up from the unknown: 'We've been getting great tapes out of England and Australia. That's what excites me: This idea that there might be somebody out there that no one's really familiar with yet that can be a new fresh face that we can exploit… in all the good ways. I think our show works so well because we don't really stunt cast. That being said, if there's some big hot TV star that's available that we love, then… As I always joke, I have my Joshua Jackson fantasy – Pacey in Mystic Falls.'

In the end, they did gamble on a virtual unknown – at least in the US. His name was Joseph Morgan, born Joseph Martin in Swansea, Wales in 1980. He studied at the Central School of Speech and Drama, which trained other acting heavyweights including Laurence Olivier and Vanessa Redgrave. Following this, he starred in a few TV movies including *Eroica* (2003) and *Henry VIII* (2003) and had a few big screen hits, too, including *Master and Commander: The Far Side of the World* (2003) with Russell Crowe and Paul Bettany and *Alexander* (2004), also starring Colin Farrell and Angelina Jolie. Most of his acting work, though, was on screens in his native UK, having shot multiple television shows including *Hex*, *William and Mary*, *Mansfield Park*, *Doc Martin* and *Casualty*. His biggest part pre-*The Vampire Diaries* was being cast in the title role in *Ben Hur*, which was shot in Morocco. No stranger to 'period' roles (as Klaus, he will surely have to act in flashbacks to different time periods) or to supernatural roles (he also stars in the upcoming film *Immortals* [2011], with Henry Cavill and Mickey Rourke), he seems a natural to play Klaus. Even Ian Somerhalder approves, saying at *Cosmopolitan* magazine's Fun

Fearless Male 2011 Awards that Joseph is, 'a magnificent guy, [whose] acting abilities are way up there.'

No doubt this will be the role to break Joseph Morgan out of the pack – and soon he'll be joining the elite rank of British-actors-turned-superhot-vampires alongside Steven Moyer (*True Blood*) and Robert Pattinson (*Twilight*). What more could any actor want?

Chapter Eleven

The Sisterhood

Caroline: Do you ever feel like there's no person in the world who loves you? (1.08, '162 Candles')

The boys might be the eye-candy in *The Vampire Diaries* but they wouldn't be anything without the amazingly strong female cast. Along with Nina Dobrev, already described by Kevin Williamson as the show's 'anchor', three other actresses bolster the show: Candice Accola, who plays Caroline Forbes, Katerina Graham (Bonnie Bennett) and Sara Canning, who plays Jenna Sommers, Elena and Jeremy Gilbert's aunt and legal guardian. They have a huge fan in Ian Somerhalder, who describes them as 'the classiest, nicest girls I've ever known.'

They must also be some of the most talented girls Ian has ever met because it seems all the girls were successful from an early age, and not just with acting. Candice Accola actually started out her career in music before she hit the big time as an actress.

Candice was born on 13 May 1987 in Houston, Texas, and grew up just outside of Orlando, Florida, in a town called Edgewood. She had two very successful parents to act as role models: her dad, Dr Kevin Accola, is a cardiothoracic (heart) surgeon and her mother, Carolyn, is a former environmental engineer who owned her own company called Accola Environmental Services, based in Orlando. Carolyn would eventually give up her job to help Candice fulfill her dreams as a singer and she formed an entertainment company (Candice Entertainment Inc.) in June 2001 to help her daughter to get a solid business going, as well as nurturing her talent.

All that investment clearly paid off! It was obvious from an early age that Candice had big ambitions. 'When I was eight or nine years old, I came home and told my mom that I was starting a girl group and that we were going to be the next Spice Girls,' she told *Orlando* magazine. The group was called Girl Zone and they sung wherever they could, from nursing homes to parties and school assemblies.

One thing was for sure: despite her parents' success – especially her mum, whose achievements as an engineer was almost unheard of for a woman – Candice never had any desire to follow in their footsteps. 'No, it wasn't my cup of tea,' she told Kidult.com, 'but I'm fascinated by their career choices and the passion they put into them. When I was younger, my mom designed landfills so for one of my science experiments, I designed miniature landfills. And whenever I go home, my little ritual is to go watch my father do surgery.'

She went to high school at Lake Highland Preparatory School, where she 'always had tons of friends and I considered myself a floater because I never belonged to a particular clique.' Indeed, it was from her high-school experience that she derived a lot of the inspiration for her 'mean girl' role in *The*

Vampire Diaries. 'In every high school there's going to be cliques... Some people are a little more snarky than others. They say one thing to your face and then another thing behind your back. I've definitely had experiences with those kinds of girls, and now I'm playing one.'

No wonder they were snarky to Candice though, as the other girls had a lot to be jealous of! A talent agent signed her up while she was in her early teens and she was writing lyrics to her own songs at fourteen. By the time she was sixteen, she was ready to move to Los Angeles and really make a go of her music career. Only six months later and she signed to Madonna's record label Maverick, home of huge stars like Alanis Morissette and Michelle Branch. For Candice and her mom, the experience was, in a word, 'Surreal! It happened quickly. That's when it resonated that if I kick my butt hard and stay positive, I can achieve what I want.'

In 2006, she dropped her first album, called *It's Always the Innocent Ones*. It had a rocky start, owing to the general downturn in the music industry due to illegal downloads and internal problems that were causing strife within the Maverick Record label itself. As a result, Candice's album was actually released by Beverly Martel Music, an independent label (for the record, she dropped her surname so she was only known as *Candice*). The album was a total flop in the United States, but that doesn't mean she wasn't a hit somewhere in the world! In fact, she found her niche in Japan, where she was named one of the top ten artists by Japanese music magazine *Burrn!* A Japanese record label called Spinning Art would later repackage her album for sale in 2008.

Success in her home country would come for Candice, but not necessarily from where she initially expected it. Living in LA, she couldn't help but be intrigued by the world of acting.

Although she had starred in a few high-school productions (she played Daisy Mae in a production of *Li'l Abner*), she really didn't have the acting bug, unlike so many of her co-stars: 'I think it would be more accurate to say I had the performing bug – I grew up performing.' In the meantime, she picked up a few acting classes to really learn the craft and felt extremely lucky to be able to start working almost right away. In 2007, she landed her first movie role in a film called *Pirate Camp*, which also starred Seth Adkins. Other bit parts followed, although some films were bigger hits than others. She loved working on *Juno* (2007) in particular: 'I was just excited to work with Ellen Page, Michael Cera and Josephine Reitman. And I heard the buzz on Diablo Cody and now I just can't get enough of her,' she told *Moving Pictures* magazine at the Toronto International Film Festival 2008, where her new movie *Deadgirl* was being screened.

Like a lot of actors in LA, Candice's career stalled during the 2007–08 actors' strike (another example was *The Vampire Diaries*' Michael Trevino, whose show was prematurely cancelled when they couldn't find writers to close out the script). In the downtime between jobs, Candice was offered an opportunity she couldn't resist: a chance to return to music. She was brought in to sing backup vocals for Miley Cyrus on her *Hannah Montana* tour. 'It was a blast!' she recalls. 'It was one of the biggest-selling tours of the decade and I got to play rock star for a little while.' Certainly, getting to run out on stage in front of 18,000 screaming fans gave her a real taste of what it would be like to be a real music superstar.

Music would always play a huge part in Candice's life, but the truth was, she had now fallen in love with acting. 'I realised how much, not only do I love the art form of acting itself, but more importantly, I love the business. It's exciting to me. I just

really love the film and television business, so I was hooked. The more I auditioned, I slowly started to work more,' she told IESB.com.

She was working, but it was mostly guest spots and background movie appearances – no big roles yet. That wouldn't happen until *The Vampire Diaries* fell onto her radar in early 2009. She went in to audition for the part of Caroline Forbes. One of Elena Gilbert's best friends, Caroline is a much more normal teenage girl than the sometimes perfect-seeming Elena, though. She gets jealous and frustrated by the attention showered upon Elena. Although Caroline is beautiful and popular in her own right, she never quite feels comfortable in her own skin – making her easy prey for bad-boy vampires like Damon. Candice threw her all into the audition and, 'I had my game face on,' she said. 'I liked Caroline, and my audition was the scene at the end of the pilot where she's talking to Bonnie about how she's never the one who gets the guy. I love that scene so much and when I read it, I was like, "Oh my goodness! I have so been there!" I've asked that question before: Why not me? Caroline is so relatable… [Getting the part] was the best feeling in the world. When you finally get that "yes" after hearing so many "no's."'

Since it really was her first big job – she had never even had a 'repeat' performance on a show before and now she had landed a lead role – Candice knew she had to knuckle down to prove to everyone she could really do this. As a character, Caroline might have seemed one- dimensional at the start, but as Season Two took off, she had a lot more development. It's what Candice likes most about her role: 'What's exciting about Caroline is that there's so much room for her to grow. And there's room for me to grow with her.' It meant, also, that she had to put her music career on the back foot – for now. In the

meantime, she's content with playing in a cover band made up of *The Vampire Diaries'* crew-members and they play at wrap parties and other *The Vampire Diaries* events!

Candice is one of the most grounded of all the actresses and her advice to others wanting to follow in her footsteps is as follows: 'Know what you want. Don't compare your accomplishments or failures to your competition and know that careers are built differently for everyone.'

Candice Accola isn't the only actress to have started out in music before joining the cast of *The Vampire Diaries*. Another was Katerina Alexandre 'Kat' Graham, who plays teenage witch Bonnie Bennett. One of the youngest cast members, Kat was born 5 September 1989. She has a very unusual multicultural background – she was born in Geneva, Switzerland, where her father, Joseph, was working as a journalist for the United Nations. Joseph Graham was born in the republic of Liberia in West Africa, bordering Sierra Leone, Guinea and the Cote d'Ivoire and went to a boarding school in England. He started out as a music executive in Liberia, where he worked with heavyweights such as Quincy Jones (he is even godfather to Quincy's two children with Peggy Lipton, and babysat Michael Jackson). When his father (Kat's grandfather) worked as a UN ambassador for Liberia to The Netherlands, Sweden, Romania and Kenya, Joseph moved out to Switzerland to work for the UN with Kat's mother, Natasha, who is Jewish with half-Russian and half-Polish heritage.

When her parents split up, Kat sometimes lived with her mum in London, sometimes in Portugal, but most often in Hollywood, California, where she was sent to Hebrew school. And the result of such an international background is a gorgeous young girl who can speak fluent English, Spanish and French along with smatterings of Portuguese and Hebrew –

she's one smart cookie! Kat also has a half-brother named Yakov, who is Israeli and from Tel Aviv. She cites her father as her inspiration in life: 'Dad is probably one of the biggest inspirations to me because he's a jazz musician – he can play the saxophone, he can play the piano. My father is pretty much the most driven man I know. I think I get a lot of my passion for life and for working and for going 110 per cent from him.'

Kat was a beautiful child and her mum got her involved in show business from the age of three, when she appeared in numerous television commercials for a variety of mainstream brands, such as K-Mart and Pop Tarts. As a result, acting never really felt like a choice that Kat made, but rather something she was born into: 'I was so young. My mom took me to auditions when I was younger and I just stuck with it, over the years. It wasn't something that I knew from when I was three years old – I don't think you can make really strong decisions at that age. It's just something that I loved to do and I had been doing it for so long that I couldn't really imagine not doing it. I grew up on set: it was like being in school or how people have their things that they've always done; it was like eating breakfast to me. I couldn't go a day without it,' she told IESB.com.

Her first big movie break came when she starred with Lindsay Lohan in the remake of the 1961 movie, *The Parent Trap*, in 1998. She was only nine years old. By 2002, she had landed another big television gig as the replacement host for singer Christina Milian on The Disney Channel show *Movie Surfers*, which looked behind-the-scenes of movie and television sets. Kat got to interview several big-name stars and was also star-struck when she interviewed Bruce Willis and Denzel Washington: 'I learned a lot – Disney really took care of me early on when I was 13, 14 to like, 16. Disney, by far, has been one of the best experiences of my life,' she told *Relate*

magazine. From her exposure on *Movie Surfers*, Kat had guest appearances on Hilary Duff's show *Lizzie McGuire*, *Malcolm in the Middle* and *Joan of Arcadia*.

Yet the multi-talented young woman wasn't only developing her acting skills, but singing, dancing and songwriting, too. It seemed Kat was destined for stardom, no matter what route she decided to pursue.

With her talent for dance, especially R&B and hip-hop styles, she was brought to the attention of Fatima Robinson, a world-famous choreographer (she has choreographed dance movies such as *Save the Last Dance* [2001] and *Dreamgirls* [2006]), who asked her to background dance at the BET Awards for rapper Lil' Bow Wow. That exposure launched her backup dancing career and she went on to dance for huge names including Jamie Fox, Gwen Stefani and Missy Elliot, and in music videos for Akon and John Legend, to name a few. Although backup dancing enabled her to tour the world and dance for a living, it's not something she would ever want to get into again: 'I literally started at the bottom. I had to stand in the way, way back of the line, learning dance moves. You have to really like days and days of rehearsals. And not just like one-hour rehearsals – from morning until night and it's exhausting: you don't get treated the same, you don't get respected the same; you don't get paid the same and it's a hassle.' Still, she idolised many dancer-singers and wanted to emulate them.

Kat had guts too, often trying to get ahead of herself in terms of auditions. One of her idols is Janet Jackson: 'I remember when I was fourteen years old I auditioned to be her backup dancer and they kicked me out because they knew I was underage. I walked right back in and they kicked me out again!' Once again, she displayed the courage and determination that was to take her far.

Acting and dance just weren't enough for Kat. There was music in her blood and lyrics, too. She wrote a song called 'Derailed', which went on to become the title track in a 2002 Jean-Claude Van Damme movie of the same name. And all this without a producer or a label. If there's anything Kat wants, she's not afraid to go out and get it herself. So if she wanted a music career, she knew she had to make it happen – and so she went out and bought the equipment she needed to mix, produce and record her own songs. She was sixteen now and still in high school but she enrolled at the Musician's Institute of Los Angeles at the same time. She earned money to support her blossoming music career by acting as one of the 'Fantanas' in a nationwide advertising campaign for Fanta drinks.

All the hard work paid off when her voice appeared on the will.i.am single 'I Got It From My Momma' (2007). It really helped her launch her music career and she launched her first single 'Boyfriend's Back' in 2009.

Though music was at the top of her priorities for a while, acting was never far behind. She did a couple of movies – *17 Again* (2009) with Zac Efron and Matthew Perry; also *Our First Christmas* (2008). Around this time, she did several pilots of TV shows for MTV, Warner Brothers and Nickelodeon, but nothing seemed to stick. 'You basically shoot these TV shows and they play them for the network and screen them. And if the network likes them, the network orders a full series or a full season. If the network doesn't like them, you'll never see them out,' she told *RelateMag*. But then in 2009 she got an audition for *The Vampire Diaries*, which she approached like any other show – with a strong sense of realism. After all, she'd been around the business long enough to know not to get her hopes up too high.

'[*The Vampire Diaries*] was just a regular audition. People

always ask me, "What made you decide to do *The Vampire Diaries*?", and I'm like, "Trust me, it wasn't my decision." Of course, I was dying to get an audition for it, but there were people that went in before me, and there were people that went in after me, all for the role of Bonnie. They liked my choices enough that they brought me back, again and again, and then I got the phone call. It's a very humbling experience, being an actor. I always want to keep it real when I talk to people about the process because I'm just one of many.'

Luckily for us, Kat got the part, which she took on with relish. Bonnie Bennett is a great role – a defining character of the show and one who helps set it apart from the likes of *Twilight*. Bonnie is a witch, although she doesn't know it for most of her life. She is descended from Salem witches and slowly comes into her powers throughout the course of the series. She has a good heart and is Elena Gilbert's best friend – the one friend Elena can trust implicitly, knowing her deepest and darkest secrets will be safe in Bonnie's hands. Throughout Season One, Bonnie never really comes to terms with the fact that her best friend is in love with a vampire, as these beings are a witch's worst enemy: 'I try to play her as real as possible and as normal as I could, and then have the discoveries, for the fans, about all her new abilities. It's so important that people can relate to her and that she's just little Bonnie Bennett, thrown into this powerful world.'

Another thing fans have recognised Kat for is her unique sense of style. She hates shopping but she loves hunting – finding clothes in vintage stores and in flea markets. Kat makes her own shoulder pieces (like bejewelled shoulder pads) and sunglasses. She loves the early 90s style: 'I am more vintage than I am high fashion. I love Lady Gaga, but I would never try and go into her lane. She's brilliant. But what I do love is

the image of Grace Jones, David Bowie and Janet Jackson. The sound of my music is 90s-dance-pop-meets-future, so I want to incorporate that in my fashion.'

Unfortunately, Kat has also experienced some of the worst consequences of fame: identity theft, especially on social networking sites such as Facebook and Twitter. Some fans become so obsessed with their favourite actor or actress that they decide to actually *become* them on those sites – deceiving other fans who aren't always able to recognise the difference: 'I have always had identity theft, in my personal life as well as my professional life, and I still get shocked by every person who does it to me; the damage that it can cause and the selfish, delusional people that take the time to do it to me. I LOVE ALL OF MY FANS and anyone that would take an interest into the work that I have made my lifelong obsession but being a fan is one thing, identity theft is another.'

It's such a shame because Kat happens to be one of the most open celebrities with her fans. She's always willing to chat and has even been known to make personal phone calls to fans if they approach her on Twitter. Her approachable nature endears her to fans and sometimes endangers her but Kat is the consummate professional and knows when not to cross the line.

More than anything, she is determined to continue making her mark on the film, television, dance and music industries. As her profile rises astronomically, she's throwing herself into all aspects of work. While other *The Vampire Diaries'* stars find it difficult to fit in further acting jobs along with their strict schedule, Kat somehow manages it with her boundless energy. She has three movies coming out in 2011 – *The Roommate* with Leighton Meister, *Boogie Town* and *Honey 2*. Just how did she find the time?

She managed this because acting is more than her passion: it's

her life. *Honey 2* was a film she had always wanted to do. She had auditioned for several dance movies and never managed to make it all the way: 'I've wanted to do a dance film for so long because I'm a dancer and it was like, "Wow, when am I going to get my chance?" I auditioned for all of the other dance movies and no one picked me and I was devastated. I finally got one and I am the lead in it, which is insane because I didn't think that would come any time soon. The director Bille Woodruff really took a chance on me and he's an incredible director and we shot it in LA with six or seven weeks of just non-stop dancing.'

The thing is, with Kat if the right role doesn't come up, she'll go ahead and *create* it. She's passionate about bringing more African-American women to American screens and she wants to write scripts to make that happen: 'I'm an extremely hands-on person. I hate to say it this way, but we're still in a time when there's not that many roles for African-American women. It's competitive. So I write a lot of scripts and try to put myself out there or I'm working on acting scripts that I've received. My manager tells me to relax. That's always gonna be a part of me, that hustler mentality. I don't want to ever rely on anyone for my career; I want to help a lot of people and I can't do that if my hands are out pleading for help.' She would love to play more serious roles one day, but is happy to wait her turn: 'Because of my age, the roles that I'm in [don't] have as much depth as I would like, but that will change. Halle Berry, Angelina Jolie, they play heavy, meaty roles, which are the sort that I want to play… [but] because of what I look like, I play with my looks, which is cool but I've done it so many times. But one day, I would love to play against my looks.'

And music will never truly take a back seat for Kat. Her latest single, 'Sassy', was released in the summer of 2010 and she

did a cover of Paula Abdul's 'Cold Hearted Snake' around that time, too. She can also be heard on *The Vampire Diaries*' soundtrack, with her cover of Garbage's 'Only Happy When It Rains'. No matter what's happening in her life, Kat Graham is going to keep on creating music.

Sara Canning is the only one out of the three supporting girls *not* to have any musical aspirations. She does, however, have a lot of acting experience and it's that experience which enables her to play a much more mature role than the others.

Sara Canning was born on 14 July 1987 in Gander, Newfoundland, Canada but quickly moved with her parents Wayne and Daphne to Sherwood Park, Alberta, near Edmonton. She found a love of performing at an early age and had an active childhood competing in figure-skating competitions and taking part in her school plays. All that acting gave her quite an overactive imagination, however, and whenever possible, she would try and sneak downstairs to watch *The X-Files* with her parents: 'I would creep into the living room and hide behind the couch to watch it… I would scare myself.'

It wasn't until she was eighteen, though, that she starred in her first professional play, George Orwell's *1984* at the Citadel Theatre in Edmonton. Despite having a great time, she knew that earning a living from acting on stage was extremely difficult. So Sara thought up a back-up plan and enrolled at the University of Alberta to study General Arts, with the possible ambition of going on to work in journalism. Still, acting was her true calling. 'Nothing really fuelled my fire the way that performing did. So I [asked myself], "Why can't I do this?"' Truth was, there was no real reason why she couldn't be a success: she had the talent – she just needed to take that courageous first step. So in 2006, aged only 19, she moved out

to Vancouver, BC and signed up for the year-long acting program at the Vancouver Film School. 'I learned a lot about the responsibility and discipline involved in working on a television series while attending Vancouver Film School,' she told *Relate* magazine. 'The program really focuses on preparing acting students for the realities of our industry.'

After graduating, she picked up an agent right away and got to work. It still wasn't easy – she had to do the stereotypical struggling-actor thing of working as a waitress in the downtime between jobs. 'It was tough at first,' she continued to *Relate*, 'pursuing what I really wanted to do while still working at a restaurant and essentially growing up very quickly.' Her first major part was in a biopic of spoilt hotel heiress Paris Hilton, titled *Paparazzi Princess: The Paris Hilton Story* (2008). Sara was cast as Nicky Hilton, Paris's handbag-designing younger sister. At first, she wasn't quite so sure of the role but she knew she couldn't be too choosy. After all, this was just a stepping stone and so she decided to throw everything into making her part in the film a success and she was surprised by what she learned: 'I watched a lot of Nicky's interviews and read up on her business endeavours, as well as lots about her relationship with Paris. But underneath the work of learning how Nicky carries herself and presents herself to people, I really tried to focus on the fact that she and Paris are sisters and they trust and rely on each other more than any other people in the whole world. That's a side of them we don't really get to see when they're getting bashed in magazines for partying too much or whatever.'

And she went back to her old film school to let them know how her first experience had gone: 'Being on set was so great, the crew was a fair size but they all worked super hard because we shot the film in a very small amount of time. Everyone was

very professional, but also really fun.' News of her success went all the way back to her former high school. Larry Frank, her drama teacher at Bev Facey High School, commented on the role to *Avenue* magazine: 'I didn't quite get it, but I thought she did a good job on it.' Meanwhile, Sara did the rounds of the Vancouver television and film scene, shooting guest spots in *Smallville* and *Kyle XY*, along with a television movie about a real-life kidnapping called *Taken in Broad Daylight* (2009).

She approached the audition for *The Vampire Diaries* with hope but no high expectations, and so she was pleasantly surprised when she got the gig. 'The stars lined up for my audition, they really did,' she told the *LA Times*. 'I was so lucky! I auditioned in Vancouver and Julie Plec [the show's co-creator] was there. I really owe so much to her and Kevin Williamson, because I think they really pushed for me. I'm so lucky it worked out.'

And she could instantly relate to her new character, Jenna Sommers, otherwise known as 'Aunt Jenna' to Elena and Jeremy Gilbert. Jenna is named the legal guardian of Elena and Jeremy after their parents (and her sister) died, but she is barely an adult herself. Still immersed in her postgraduate studies, she's smart but flustered and undone by the sudden duty of being a parent: 'Jenna suddenly had to shoulder all of this responsibility and, essentially, grow up all at once and I can relate to that. She has flaws that she's working out, but she has such a good heart. She wants to do the most noble job she can of taking care of Elena and Jeremy after their parents' death. She's helping them through this difficult phase of being in high school with boys and drugs and vampires, but she's also got school and her own life to worry about.'

Initially, Sara found it strange to be cast in the 'adult' role, especially as she was only a year or so older than Nina Dobrev

(Elena) and Steven R. McQueen (Jeremy) and also much younger than Paul Wesley (Stefan) or Ian Somerhalder (Damon). By being especially careful with how they dress her and do her make-up, the stylists on *The Vampire Diaries'* set are able to make Sara look and feel older than she really is and to give her that (often wavering) air of authority.

The pilot was filmed in her hometown of Vancouver so Sara really didn't have to travel far. She didn't even know for sure whether the show would take off: 'When I did the pilot, I knew, of course, that there was a huge vampire fascination right now, but I guess we weren't really sure how the show would be received.' In the meantime, she signed up to do another project: a movie role that has most helped her to grow as an actress. She was cast as Maggie McGregor in the independently-made feature *Black Field* (2009), a historical drama set in the nineteenth century about two Scottish sisters struggling to build a life on the Canadian prairies: 'The character, Maggie, was so complex and had as many interesting flaws as strengths. Reading the script, her motivations were sometimes hard to understand, making for a very dynamic story. While developing her character and determining her arc in the film, I became very aware of the specificities needed in each scene. I learned a lot from that process!' The director of the film, Danishka Esterhazy, had nothing but great things to say about Sara: 'Sara is an incredibly intelligent actor. She came to town so prepared and had done so much of her own research on dialect and history. She really was completely ready for the role.'

Luckily, Sara had just wrapped the movie when she was asked to come back to work full-time on *The Vampire Diaries*. Late in the summer of 2009, she moved down to Atlanta, Georgia – a city with a completely different vibe to Vancouver: 'It's definitely a much different culture than the West Coast of

Canada, but everyone's been really friendly. I really like it here. It was really different at first, and Canada will always be home, but this has become like my second home. Everyone I have worked with has turned it into a family – it's been fantastic.' She shares her Atlanta apartment with Nina Dobrev, where they make each other coffee and go over the script. 'It's a little eerie, how everyone really genuinely loves each other,' she said.

Now Sara is fully entrenched in *The Vampire Diaries* and one of the best-loved characters in the show – even as she remains probably the only main character who doesn't know about the vampires! Surrounded by all the fascinating people in the cast and crew, Sara developed ambitions to try other areas of the film/television industry: 'I'm completely interested in all other aspects of the industry. As a storyteller, I would love to be able to direct or watch something that I've written.' She is in the middle of developing a script, describing it as 'a collision of a few different genres', mixing the current fascination with Westerns with a love story and fantasy. Sounds fascinating!

Chapter Twelve

A Dream of London

Stefan: I lost control today. Everything I've kept buried inside came rushing to the surface. I'm simply not able to resist her. (1.01, 'Pilot')

The Vampire Diaries has altered the course of Paul Wesley's life forever. It has skyrocketed him to a stratosphere of fame all actors dream of but few really attain. While at the moment his time is tied up by the show, there's no question that when it comes to an end, he will have become a huge star with the world at his feet. When asked by the *Miami Herald* how *The Vampire Diaries* had changed his life, Paul replied: 'I can't sum up into a short enough answer for you but in one word, I'd have to say very surreal, in a good way.'

In the past he has shared how much he would like to star in feature films and in the summer of 2010, he actually had the opportunity to star in one such film. Alright, it wasn't the big-budget Hollywood blockbuster he had been waiting for, but it was a fun, straight-to-DVD release that had a good message at its

heart. Plus, he got to film in the Caribbean Sea – who wouldn't want that?

The film was called *Beneath the Blue* (previously titled *Way of the Dolphin*) and it was inspired by real-life events in the Bahamas. Paul played Craig Forrester, a young naval officer sent out to investigate the disappearance of a dolphin. While out there he meets a research scientist (played by young actress Caitlin Wachs), who has developed an artificial way of communicating with dolphins through clicks. The story follows their relationship as they delve deeper into the mystery of the missing dolphin, leading to a discovery that the US Navy's sonar testing might be killing whales and dolphins. This was an actual court case that reached the US Supreme Court.

A smaller role that might impact his future was Paul's part in *24*. He played Jack Bauer's son-in-law, husband to Kim (played by Elisha Cuthbert) and shot his scenes just before landing the part of Stefan, but they aired almost simultaneously – giving him even more exposure. But fans wanted to know, was there a chance of seeing more Paul on *24*? 'Not that I'm aware of,' he told the *Los Angeles Times*. 'I'd auditioned for [*24*] so many times over the years, and one day this character came about and they offered it to me, without an audition. I said "Absolutely." When we shot my first two episodes of *24*, I didn't even know that I had *Vampire Diaries*. I love the show, I'm a huge fan, and I think the acting is so good. The writers are great. If they were to expand the character, and I could make time for it, it'd be fantastic.'

In fact, Paul did end up on the show again – in early 2010: 'It was a pleasure to work on the show because it's such a prestigious show and I just wanted to be involved in any way possible. I love Elisha. She's so sweet and I got to meet Kiefer Sutherland [who plays Jack Bauer], which is great because I'm

a big fan.' It was a special privilege to meet Kiefer, as he knows as well as anyone what it's like to make your name as a vampire! One of his first big roles was in the famous 1980s teen vampire flick *Lost Boys* – often credited with giving vampires their cool, handsome edge.

Paul's shows led to other good consequences, too – romantic ones, for instance. On the set of *Killer Movie* (2008), he got to meet his now-fiancée Torrey DeVitto. Like everything in the acting world, it seems, there is a strange symmetry in the fact that Paul and Torrey are together. After all, she got her big break working on the second sequel to the Kevin Williamson-penned film, *I Know What You Did Last Summer*, called *I'll Always Know What You Did Last Summer* (2006). Like Paul, she also did modelling work for Ford Modeling Agency and agreed that it wasn't for her.

Killer Movie was a comedy-horror film that also starred *Gossip Girl*'s Leighton Meester. These days Torrey is best known for her role on The CW's *One Tree Hill* and Alloy Entertainment's latest production, *Pretty Little Liars*. Paul certainly seems extremely smitten and even joked to the press that they were already married (probably something he shouldn't joke too much about as a lot of fans took his word as gospel and were very upset to have their favourite heart-throb suddenly taken officially off the market!). But with her Kevin Williamson connection and close ties to The CW, maybe we will see Torrey on *The Vampire Diaries* one day.

For now, the couple have to be content with a long-distance relationship. Although they are very much in love, they also have to focus on building their careers, something that often takes them in very different directions. For now, Torrey is living and working in LA, while Paul continues filming several thousand miles away in Atlanta, Georgia. However, Torrey is

used to the showbiz lifestyle and knows how to juggle relationships. Her father was drummer for Billy Joel for almost 30 years, 'So he was constantly on tour and I always travelled growing up. It's kind of been a way of life for me, so it's rather fitting that is the way things are now. And when you get into this business, you know that anything can be thrown at you at any time, you just have to go with the flow.'

What Torrey might not be so comfortable with is the level of female fan attention that Paul receives! It's the same for every teenage heart-throb; their girlfriends are subject to quite a lot of jealousy – just look at the frenzy over are-they-or-aren't-they Robert Pattinson and Kristen Stewart. But *The Vampire Diaries'* fans are much more considerate than *Twilight* fans, and Torrey considers herself very lucky: 'I haven't had any 14-year-old girls try to take me out yet, so that's a good thing. I think it's endearing and cute, and embrace the whole thing.'

At the moment, *The Vampire Diaries* takes up all of Paul's time but, like any other actor, he has at least one dream role in mind: 'Holden Caulfield – *Catcher in the Rye* changed my life when I was a kid. I read it as I was a boy turning into a man and I was so fascinated by the values: I believe in it. Of course, I'll never play him because J.D. Salinger will never allow anyone to play him. To be honest with you, if I were offered the part I might be too terrified to accept but in my perfect world, that's who I would play.' Even since J.D. Salinger's death on 28 January 2010, his estate has remained reluctant to allow a film adaptation of his masterpiece, so Paul is unlikely to get his chance.

The desire to play such a literary icon taps into the other side of Paul's ambition. His other passion – and possible career option – has been in writing and directing. As far back as his *Fallen* days, Paul has spoken of a desire to get behind the camera, as well as out front: '[Directing an episode of *Fallen*] is

like my dream! I'm writing a film right now. I think most actors have that aspiration. I think directing and writing and acting all inter-twine and you should do what you're not used to doing. If you play the same character all the time it's gonna be boring, I just want to create stuff.' In between acting, at the age of twenty, he actually did get pretty far in his own creative project: putting together a documentary with his friends about the story of Clifford Etienne, a boxer who started out his career while in prison. 'We're going to interview him and his family, and we have footage of him fighting,' Paul said. 'We hope to sell it [the documentary] to film festivals.'

He also likes the idea of being an investigative journalist and it's easy to see why. Paul enjoys getting under the skin of a person or an issue, exploring why choices are made and discovering something unexpected or revealing. For the moment, *The Vampire Diaries* will have to fill that creative outlet for him. Luckily for him, Kevin Williamson and Julie Plec are open to having their actors make suggestions: 'As a matter of fact, when we get the scripts, we have a relationship where we can call them and say, "Why do I do this?" Julie and Kevin write our characters for us and the way that we play our characters, they'll see something and go, "Oh, I like that smile there," or "I like Stefan sort of sinister," and they start writing more of that. They cater to it and, in a sense, mould it to your liking,' he told IESB.com.

For now, we just have to settle for seeing him in the role of Stefan from *The Vampire Diaries*. '[I have] no firm plans yet,' Paul told WetPaint.com, 'but when we're on hiatus I'd like to play someone very different from Stefan – the opposite. Right now, the priority is the show, though if the right thing comes about, I'll try and do it. I would like to write screenplays, too. A friend of mine wrote a script a while ago and we ended up raising the

money and putting on a play in LA, which I was in, and that was great. So we've written another screenplay together and I'd like to do something with that. As regards long-term ambitions for me, I'd like to live in Europe. So many cities appeal but London, I think, is really cool.'

That's one reason why acting suits him so well – Paul is addicted to the uncertainty, the spontaneity and the risks involved. What he loves about his career is 'the same thing that makes me nervous, which is never knowing what will happen next. That's what I love about it. I never know what character I'm going to play next, I never know what location I'll be in next – with each new character, I find something new about myself that I didn't know before.'

Chapter Thirteen

Epilogue

You wake up back in your bedroom, and you're all alone. Have you been dreaming? Memory is foggy; time seems to have slipped past without your notice… weren't you just in a graveyard?

You feel different, changed. Stepping out of bed, you pass by the mirror on your dressing table. Wait a moment, what's that on your neck?

It's a chain… leading to a beautiful, ornate pendant filled with some kind of herb. Immediately you recognise it: vervain.

Stefan was here, after all.

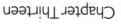